Contents

GW00356926

Introduction

OFTEN we are unaware of the history that surrounds us. When looking at Hampshire, for instance, we tend to see only the charming villages, the market towns, the river valleys, the downs, the sea, the wide open spaces. We are not always conscious of the people who were here before us.

This book is an attempt to rectify that. I have selected a few incidents from around the county, setting each in a different historical period, and tried to give a fictional impression of what it was like to be alive at that time. The events I have described are based on fact, although most of the characters are from my imagination – except, of course, those who can be found in formal books of history. In this way I hope to illuminate the long past of this diverse and interesting region.

I have been greatly helped both by friends and professional historians and I thank them all – as I do the staff of the many museums I have visited, the local librarians and those at study centres and historical sites. Without their knowledge and advice my task would have been very much harder.

I hope you enjoy the book as much as I have its writing.

HAMPSHIRE HISTORIES

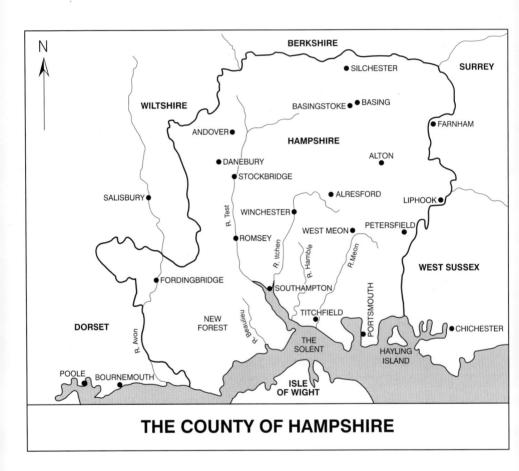

THE COUNTY OF HAMPSHIRE

HAMPSHIRE HISTORIES

by

JOAN HAINES

MEON VALLEY BOOKS

By the same author:

1996. *Beside the Meon: A Journey Through Time*

Illustrations by Shirley Whiting
Cover photograph by Glynn Williams

© Joan Haines, 1999.

Published by Meon Valley Books,
Meonside, East Meon, Hants, GU32 1PD.

ISBN 0-9527687 - 1 - 2

Cover photograph of Old Winchester Hill, showing
three Bronze Age round barrows and
Iron Age ramparts.

Maps are hand-drawn and are not to scale.

Printed in England by: P.P.G. Design & Print Ltd.,
Hilsea, Hampshire.

Chapter One

Petersfield, 1400 B.C.

The morning was fine. Mer stood in the opening of the roundhouse and yawned. The babies had cried a lot in the night and she had slept badly, as had Pen. He had been out in the fields for some time now and she could see him ploughing with the two oxen. That was hard work, the ard being heavy and unwieldy, and he would need hot gruel when he came in, for although there had not been a frost in the night, the dawn was chilly.

Taking up some dry twigs she fed them carefully into the embers of yesterday's fire. The eventual reward was a curl of smoke followed by a small flame. As she knelt on the damp, cold earth of the floor, Pen's father awoke. He stumbled out of the house to the area they used as a latrine, followed by his mother, who pulled a skin from the sleeping place and draped it round her shoulders. If they had been much disturbed in the night they would now be surly and unhelpful, and she dreaded that. Both were old, she knew, but that was no reason to obstruct Pen in his new plans for the farming. Were they jealous, perhaps? Jealous of his ability to change from the old ways and be willing to adopt the new? Old people did not trust change.

The light from the hut opening was momentarily obscured as the Father re-entered. He came to the fire holding out a pottery mug.

"The gruel's not hot yet," Mer apologised. "I've not been up long."

Grunting in reply he dropped the mug on the ground, careless of whether it broke or not, and went out again. She knew now what to expect. The Mother would be as bad. However, the older woman did not return and Mer guessed she was already in the working-house, continuing the cutting of cattle hides. Although the beasts had been slaughtered at the end of the year, the hides still smelt. They had not been fully dried out before the wet weather had come, so the pegs, which stretched them on the ground, had been removed too early. Since then there had been too much rain to peg them out again and the Mother was now working with very inferior leather. Even for shoes it was poor. Still, the warmer weather could not be far off and the family could all go barefoot again.

The baby woke then, so she fed her at the breast while she threw a few handfuls of coarsely ground wheat into a pot of water heating on the fire. Squatting now, with the baby resting on her knees while it suckled, she stirred the gruel with a peeled stick. The Mother did not like lumps and the Father spat them out, making the hut floor slippery until the dogs came to eat the mess. When the older child woke he was put on the other breast but she knew that milk alone would not be enough for him. She would have to wet some ground wheat grains, form them into flat rounds and bake them on the hot hearth-stone. Her bread was always gritty and often ash covered, but at least the family was fed.

Eventually, after pushing several large stones from the nearby pile into the embers to heat for the later cooking, she was ready to begin work. Tying the smallest baby into a woven cloth and slinging this round her shoulders, she put the older child on her hip and went out to join Pen and the Father in the fields. These were small and square but had to be cross-ploughed to break up the soil sufficiently for seed-sowing. Her job that morning was to follow Pen and the ard and throw into a heap any big stones he turned up. The Father would then put them into a wicker basket, carry this to the edge of the field and tip out the stones. It was in this way that the banks surrounding the ploughland had been made. Eventually some were high enough to keep out the cattle which otherwise wandered across the new-sown wheat.

After some time Pen stopped the ploughing, rested the oxen, and led the way back to the roundhouse. When once again in the darkness of the hut, Mer laid down the children and filled various beakers with the now hot gruel, taking one to the Mother who was still at work on the skins.

"Has it got lumps?" the woman asked "I can't abide them."

Reassured on this point, she sipped carefully, straining the fluid through the gaps in her teeth. Satisfied, she went on with her cutting, using a sharp-edged flint knife.

"What is the leather for this time?" Mer asked pleasantly.

"Belts," came the answer. "Belts for Pen and the Father."

Pleased that she had at least been answered, Mer returned to the main hut. She must put the stew on now otherwise there would be no midday meal. Taking a wooden platter, she fetched from one of the storehouses nearby the remaining portions of a wild pig. This had been dismembered by the Father the day before and the joints strung from the rafters to cure in the smoke from the central cooking fire. Today she took the head and feet, setting them in a large cooking pot with plenty of water from the stream. The fire had sunk quite low so she knew it was useless to try cooking over it. She did not wish to pile on more wood for, at this end of winter, fuel was short. Instead she knocked out from the embers several of the now red-hot stones she had placed there earlier, and managed to drop them one by one into the pot. Gradually the water heated up and, by adding more and more stones every few minutes, the meat cooked. The task was tedious but such pot-boilers saved a great deal of firewood.

In between tending both the fire and her children, she was able to make a meal for the next day. The guts of the pig had already been cleaned and put to soak in salted water, and Mer now lifted these out. On the flat hearthstone she chopped up the pig's liver, lights and brain, then, with fat from the stomach lining, she mixed everything together with a few of last year's poppy seeds for flavour. The guts she then stuffed as best she could and tied the ends with supple stems of wild bryony. The result she laid aside for boiling when the pig's head was done.

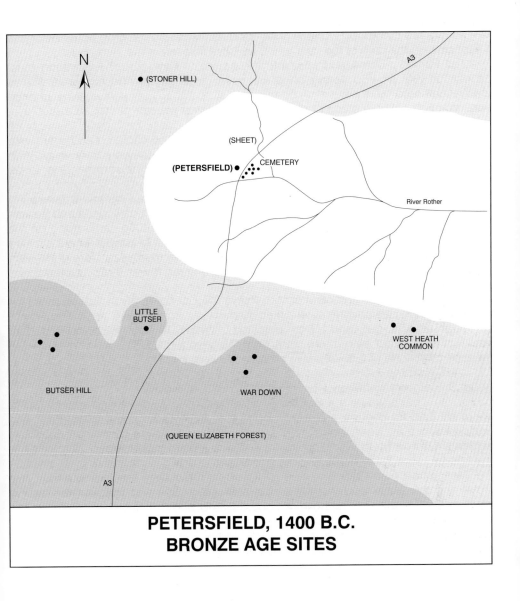

N

● (STONER HILL)

(SHEET)

(PETERSFIELD) ● CEMETERY

A3

River Rother

LITTLE
BUTSER
●

WEST HEATH
COMMON
●   ●

●   ●
●

WAR DOWN
●   ●
●

BUTSER HILL

(QUEEN ELIZABETH FOREST)

A3

**PETERSFIELD, 1400 B.C.
BRONZE AGE SITES**

That evening the family sat in the roundhouse, the gloom lightened only by the fire's glow and the pale light from the last of the day that came through the door opening.

"I was thinking, Father," Pen began, "of planting some of these new beans our neighbours are trying out. Our soil is as good as theirs and the crop could be useful – especially in the cold of the year when we have little left in the storehouse."

The Father grunted and spat into the embers. "New crops? Everything must be new, is that it? You young ones are never content with the old ways. We've always gathered wild peas and beans and stored them for winter. Why change that? Wasting a whole piece of ploughland on a crop we can gather so easily? No, I say. No!"

Pen sighed. Always his ideas were blocked. "But the cattle could be fed with them, too," he added. "Before the grass sprouts in spring they are very weak. With beans they would be stronger – and breed better. We would be stronger, too, for as a field crop we would harvest more."

Mer could see he was not hopeful of agreement but knew he had to make the effort. He had watched other families in the settlement try out new ideas and he was both angry and frustrated by his inability to copy them. Putting cattle dung on the ploughland had been another idea but the Father had said to leave it where it fell on the grass of the pasture. Mer had heard Pen explain that there was more grass than ploughland and so plenty for the cattle to eat each year. It was the cultivated crops that were of prime importance.

The Mother then stirred and asked, "Have the Overlords given their consent for these changes? Has anyone even asked them?"

"Our land is our land," Pen objected. "When the Overlords divided their holdings among our clan, there were no rules attached – save that of recognising them as chiefs. We can do what we wish on our own soil."

"Ah!" said the Mother. "Not so! You forget the power of the Ancestors, buried under those great white mounds, gleaming on the hills above us. That is where the power lies. That is where the Gods are, too. The Overlords merely gave each family some hill land for pasture and some fertile land for crops. I know it was they who decided where the boundaries should go, who should dig the ditches around each settlement, throw up the dividing banks and who placed palisades on their tops but their power lay with the Gods and the Ancestors."

Mer sighed. She knew that the Mother would now talk at length about the Long Dead and the Gods, and would not be interrupted. She was thankful the babies were asleep for their crying now would bring only anger. It was better to hear the Mother in patience and keep the peace.

"When I was young," the older woman began, "we held the Ancestors in honour and sought their approval of our deeds. They were nearer to the Gods than we and so knew what was best for us. My father's father told me of these things when I was small and I have never forgotten them. In early days, he said, settlements had been fewer and dwellings merely scattered among the fields. More men went hunting than now, the wild beasts being many, but although the kin lived far apart they always owed allegiance to their Overlords. And at that time the Overlords were hugely rich and had much gold interred with their bodies in their long, long graves – not round, like ours. The Sky Gods had still been worshipped then, you see, and due honour was paid by giving them the weapons, the wonderful and decorative ornaments, and the tools of the chieftains. Sometimes these things were broken or spoilt before being placed in the burial chambers for, in this way, the items were known to have been truly given as they were no longer of use to men."

She cleared her throat, for the fire smoke was thick that night. "But now," she went on in disgust, "men give few gifts of that kind. They keep their precious things for their own use, or even have the gold and bronze of the dead melted down by the smiths and remodelled. Such doings are not good. The Gods will punish us for sure. In those old days, you must understand, a man's wealth was shown by the gifts he left to the Gods when dead. Nowadays his greatness depends on the amount of land and treasure he holds when living. That can't be right. It can't be right."

As she subsided into silence, Mer glanced at the Father and saw that he was asleep. She knew that if Pen could convert the Mother to his way of thinking, the old man would eventually be won over. So she nodded and made a small gesture of encouragement with her hand.

Pen began quietly. "But you see, Mother, we don't bury our dead like that now. Do we? You were with us at the funeral rites of the last great warrior chief. His body was burnt, you'll remember. Burnt, and his ashes put in a pottery urn, the lid pressed over, and the whole laid in a pit within the round mound built to cover it. Without a body to bury, the reverence given to an Overlord changed and he was allowed to lie in a single grave with none of the clan added later. For this reason, it seems to me, the reverence done him was the greater. To lie alone, under a gleaming white and chalky tomb, is a sign of power and splendour and of honour to the Gods. Don't you agree? Times change, Mother, and we have to do things differently." Cautiously he smiled at her. "Like with planting beans in the fields?"

The old woman snorted. "You won't get round me like that!" she said. "I am old and like the old ways. You won't change me!"

"But your father's father changed," Mer commented gently. "You've just told us of the times when settlements were few and scattered. And I've heard you say that in those days there were no enclosures like we have – though how they kept the cattle and other beasts out of the fields I don't know."

"In the very long past our peoples didn't have fields! They wandered the land, as I've said. There were not even proper trackways like now."

"There you are, Mother!" Pen cried triumphantly. "Things change!"

Mer shook her head at him. His eagerness was all too likely to upset her again. "Tell us about when you were young," she suggested, "when your parents died and you were left to tend the farm. That was hard work on your own, I'm sure."

The mother cast her a wry smile and Mer knew she was not fooled by the change of tone. However, she did agree to speak of that time.

"It was hard work such as you've no idea of," she said. "The ploughing was the worst – my back has never been the same since." She sighed and then went on, "Having two great men to do it for you, you won't know how strong you have to be to hold an ard half on its side. Unless I did that, you see, the cutting point was likely to slip over the surface of any hard ground, not loosening the soil ready for the seed. On a sloping field the strain was terrible – even the Father has difficulty with that. You've seen his crooked shoulders? All due to the ard. And I dare say Pen will be the same later on." She paused for a moment. "The cross-ploughing was easier, of course, because the main soil was already broken. It's because of the cross-ploughing our fields are small and square. I'd never try an ard on one of the grass fields we use for pasturing the animals. That needs a man's strength. To turn the grass, that is. But harvesting wheat is also back-breaking but I had to do that, too, in those days. There was no one else."

She gave a small laugh and went on, "But I tell you, I could handle that bronze sickle with real speed, cutting the sheaves at ground level. But when my back failed me I had to hold a bundle of stalks higher, near the ears, and just slice them off, dropping them into a basket for winnowing later. Ah! it was a hard life, I tell you, and I was truly glad when the Father offered for me, even though he was a little too close in kinship for my liking. Still, it did mean that we both stayed in our own settlement. I wouldn't have liked to go away to another, as they sometimes did in the old days."

Mer looked at the Mother with new interest. After such a life she surely had every right to be fierce and cross when the babies kept her awake. She was old, but she was tough and was due respect from those younger.

After a little silence the Mother spoke again. "It was having the Ancestors within sight all day that kept me strong. Up in the hills, under their great mounds. It felt safer to be near them, for surely they gave protection to our clan. And still do. Without those Great Warriors and the Gods to overlook us, we are too much alone."

She glanced at Pen and then at Mer. "That is something you young ones don't understand. You put too much faith in yourselves. You think your greatness depends on landowning and beautiful treasures of bronze and gold that you keep for your own use. You've even begun to exchange your extra goods for such things! I've heard, too, of a bronze shield of wondrous design that came from trading with a stranger from the south. And of new pots of a different design and of a clay better than that from here! It's all change now. And I don't like it! I'm happier with the old ways."

She sighed. "But don't forget the Gods. I think the seasons have become colder and wetter in recent years because of your neglect of worship. In the old days the winter sun was said to be warmer and the birds mated earlier. There were fewer losses among the cattle-young in those days – whereas now they shiver in the rain and die of cold. I tell you, change is not good. It mocks the Gods."

When she had finished speaking, both Pen and Mer remained silent. Never before had they heard the Mother talk in such a way.

"I shall die soon," the old woman went on. "And when I do, I want my ashes to be scattered before the house doorway. In that way I shall always be here – and always in sight of those great round tombs on the hill."

"But the beans mother?" Pen asked desperately. "May we not change enough to plant those? To spread dung on the fields? To sow barley as well as wheat? To keep more sheep for their wool? Must we stay in the past forever – just to please the Gods?"

There was a long silence, after which she shook her head. "I do not know. You must ask the Father and he must ask the leaders of our clan. If they give permission then I say you may do these things." Then, speaking more loudly and in a voice full of scorn, "I don't suppose either Pen or the Father will have a mound over their ashes here in the cemetery – for they're not important enough. They're just small farmers and count for little in the settlement. So they'll just be scattered, like the unconsidered of the clan."

At that the old man stirred. "I have been awake this long while," he said. "But while I slept the Gods sent me a dream and in that dream I became a leader myself.

And I was a leader because I brought new riches to the clan by doing all those things that Pen has suggested." Then he turned to the Mother and added in a fierce voice, "I did not like the things you said about my being unconsidered in the clan and not having a round tomb with a buried urn! I shall soon be of sufficient importance for that, you'll see! Never will my ashes be so unimportant that I am merely scattered to the winds. So remember that, woman! And treat me with a greater respect."

Then he looked at Pen "Tomorrow we plough a new plot from the pasture and sow beans. Can you find some?"

"Yes, yes!" Pen replied eagerly. "Hoping for such a decision I exchanged two hens for a bagful. Tomorrow we can begin to be rich!"

The old Mother looked sideways at Mer and gave a small and secret smile.

Based on:

"Wessex to AD 1000" by Barry Cunliffe. Longman, 1993.

"Iron Age Farm: The Butser Experiment" by Peter J. Reynolds. British Museum Publications, 1979.

"Bronze Age Metalwork in Southern Britain" by Susan M. Pearce. Shire Archaeology, 1984.

"Food & Cooking in Prehistoric Britain" by Jane Renfrew. English Heritage, 1985.

"Women in Prehistory" by Margaret Ehrenberg. British Museum Publications, 1992.

"Ancient Agricultural Implements" by Sian Rees. Shire Archaeology, 1981.

"The Social Foundations of Prehistoric Britain" By Richard Bradley. Longman, 1984.

"Prehistoric Houses in Britain" by Malcolm L. Reid. Shire Archaeology, 1993.

"Hampshire Treasures Survey" (Volume Six, East Hampshire). Hampshire County Council, 1982.

Wall Displays in Petersfield Museum.

Main Bronze Age Barrows near Petersfield (Ordnance Survey, Section SU)

On the Heath	756 231	*West Heath Common*	783 226
			788 225
Butser Hill	714 202		
	715 208	*War Down, Buriton*	728 198
	716 202		
		Clanfield	715 170
Little Butser	719 207		716 166
		Charlton	734 156
Settlement site	717 181		
	(Now beneath road)		

Chapter Two

Danebury Hillfort, 350 B.C.

K ran swung his bag of tools onto his other shoulder. His equipment was heavy and he had walked all day. Bronzeworking was his life but, moving from camp to camp as he did, it was a hard life and often wearisome. Now the long hill slope which led to the settlement was before him and he braced himself for the climb. Despite his being only of nineteen summers, he was becoming very tired.

As he approached the eastern gateway he saw the defensive outworks had recently been strengthened – and wondered why. Had he arrived at a time of war? Was there a new leader, keen on attacking others or one who was fearful of others attacking him? Or a chief intent on displaying his power and prestige by raising the height of the ramparts and the depth of their outer ditches? Now he was too tired to worry.

As he passed through the first opening in the great banks, he called to the spearholders lounging behind the palisades on their tops. "Greetings! I am Kran the bronzeworker and come in peace. I seek shelter for the night and a place to set up my fire."

Before the men were ready to wave him through they asked him to tell them from where he had come and what news he carried. Resignedly, he lowered his pack to the ground and eased his shoulders.

"Many days have I walked," he told them. "I come from near the Great Sea but now there is little work for me there, for others dealing in iron have moved in and have taken my trade. So I followed the river called Bourne until I saw ramparts on the hills above me, and then I climbed – as I have had to here. But the fort known as Figsbury was abandoned, except for a few herdsmen and their sheep. So I went to the hill called Quarley, but this camp was empty, too. I did not know why. It was hard to find food, as you can imagine, but a few farmers fed me in exchange for gossip and a little repair work to their ornaments and horse-tackle. Then I left the riverside and went towards the rising sun. I had been told to look for a settlement on Bury Hill but there I suffered an attack by its few occupants from a hail of sling shot. And now I'm here."

"You are welcomed," one of the men told him. "We are doing well here and are rich. Our fort is now the greatest on this ridge and many have come to us from

Figsbury and Quarley, but not yet from Bury. We hold land to far distances and have much power. Our chief is the king of all you can see."

Kran smiled in admiration. He picked up his leather bag and swung it on his shoulder again. "May I now pass? I need shelter for the night."

The men waved him through. "And don't forget," one called, "you'll need to ask permission from our king to set up work. He'll no doubt need gifts in exchange. But beware of Tollith. He's the king's favourite craftsman and an ironworker – and very jealous of his rights."

Raising a hand in grateful acknowledgement, Kran entered the enclosure. Being near the day's end, much cooking was being done in the circular houses, most of which were placed near one of the ramparts for protection from the weather, for the wind and rain could drive wildly across a hilltop. Now, however, the calm of dusk was over the settlement and he could see the first stars glimmering. Slowly, so that he might be well noted by the inhabitants, he walked the length of the central road, his tired feet awkward on the cobbles. Reaching the four holy sanctuaries, plank-built and straw-thatched, he paused. Out of deference to the gods of these people he raised his bag of tools and bowed low, offering his craftsmanship to the deities. Then he took a side path and passed among the dwellings, asking for lodging. The smell from the cooking pots gave him a great hunger.

A household led by Dod, a potter, accepted him for the night in exchange for long talk and a promise to repair a crack in a bronze vessel. Kran ate well that evening and, with the comfort of a full belly, his sleep was sound. At daybreak the family broke their fast on hot gruel and flat barley cakes, Dod's children having livened the fire with the aid of leather bellows. After the sparse meal Kran thought about seeking out the chief of the settlement to gain permission to work. Before he could do this, however, the woman of the house set him to doing his share of the daily grind of spelt wheat on the hand quern, the children scraping the resultant flour into a pottery bowl, no doubt made by Dod. This done, the chief's house was pointed out to him and he set off with his tools to meet him.

He found a tall man, neither young nor old, talking to a warrior dressed in the finery of a noble. Kran laid down his toolbag and touched both hands to his forehead in obeisance. "Chief," he said, "I am come in peace from afar, seeking only to work with bronze to the benefit of your people. I am skilled in casting to make horse trappings and linchpins for the axles of chariot wheels, rings for your sword belts and bosses for your shields. I am a metalworker of renown. My name is Kran."

The warrior pulled his long moustaches and glanced at the noble beside him. "Do we need such a man?" he asked. "Now that we have iron, bronze is of less importance."

"If he can do sheetwork he'd be of use," was the reply.

"My lord, I can work sheet bronze! Naturally! My only lack is sufficient of the metal to hammer out. Given a good supply of bronze, particularly that from the land towards the setting of the winter sun, I could make you prestige sword sheaths, cauldrons, shields, decorative caps for your war horses. Am I not Kran, the bronzeworker?"

"So," the Chief mused. "You have little metal with you?"

"I have a few objects already made, some good sized pieces of scrap, and a bag of filings. These I use for repair work and the creation of small items. Already I have found your potter, Dod, in need of my skill and there must be many others.

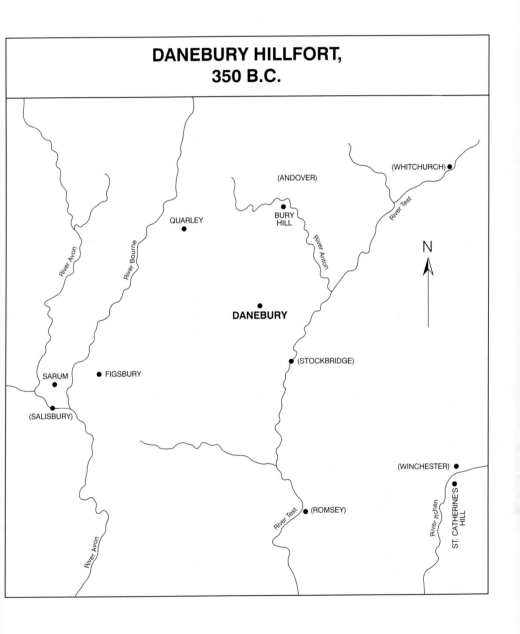

DANEBURY HILLFORT,
350 B.C.

(WHITCHURCH) ●

(ANDOVER)

River Test

QUARLEY ●

BURY
HILL ●

River Anton

River Avon

River Bourne

N

● DANEBURY

● (STOCKBRIDGE)

SARUM
●

● FIGSBURY

● (SALISBURY)

(WINCHESTER) ●

●
ST. CATHERINE'S
HILL

River Itchen

River Test ● (ROMSEY)

River Avon

The settlement would benefit." As the chief was silent, Kran went on, "And my work for you, my lord, I would give for no fee."

The leader nodded. "I agree, to your request," he said. "It is some time since a bronzeworker was here. We have Tollith, a master craftsman in iron who sees to most of our needs, but none of your trade. You may stay."

Again Kran touched his hands to his forehead and left. With a light heart he returned to Dod's hut where he set about repairing the cracked vessel as he had promised. Then he went in search of Tollith to make his peace with him so as to avoid enmity. All craftsmen were jealous of their skills, and iron, Kran had to admit, was a stronger and more useful metal than bronze and could be nearly as decorative. But old fashioned bronze was what he used and he would not now change.

Tollith's workshop lay in the area where the tall ramparts would cast a cooling shadow over the smith's furnace at summer noontime. "Master!" the young man called. "Greetings! I am Kran, a worker in bronze, who has been granted leave to work here."

"Oh, yes?" the other said, continuing to hammer a piece of metal.

After a moment Kran went on, "I'm told you are a great craftsman – a wonder-worker in iron." As there was no response he added. "And greatly admired by the king and his nobles. And by the warriors for the making of their horse gear."

Tollith laid down his hammer. "I am busy. Can you not see? I have no time to talk."

"Then I leave you, Master," Kran replied as peaceably as he could, being determined not to annoy the man. Receiving not even a nod in acknowledgement, he walked away in irritation. He had not deserved such treatment. Metalworkers in both iron and bronze were highly esteemed. Socially, they counted above all farmers and even above the lesser nobles, especially those who were not part of the king's inner circle. Without metalwork no society could thrive – the people would have to return to the primitive flint or wooden implements of the Ancients. Also he, Kran, was an expert in adding the final decorations to what would otherwise be mere utilitarian items of no real beauty. It was he, and those like him, who produced the great neck torcs, the arm rings, the razors, the thorn tweezers, the bridle decorations and the scabbard bindings and who could add sumptuous inlays of coral or enamel. If ironworking was the necessary task, bronzeworking made it fit for the gods. Both crafts should be equally respected.

Defiantly, Kran retrieved his bag from Dod's hut. Now he would create an object of such beauty that his worth could be more than proved to Tollith. Perhaps he would make four bronze buttons, decorated with rosettes for the tunic of the king. Or a hubcap, fit for the chariot of the grandest warrior. Or a buckle of such intricate design that none could fathom its making. He chose a working site well away from Tollith and behind the storage buildings which lined much of one of the roads. There he took from his bag a lump of beeswax, dirty now from much use, and began to mould it in his hands. The gods would let him know what he should make.

Gradually his anger eased and he found he was forming a model of a raven as long as his thumb. A raven was a magical bird that carried omens in its wings. Sure now of his intentions, he left his belongings beneath the nearest six-post granary building and set off to look for clay. The settlement and its ramparts lay on chalk, but he knew from his travels of the day before that clay was visible in the lower valley. He found what he needed without difficulty and retraced his steps. Taking up his raven again he carefully coated it with the damp clay, making sure that a small hole was made in the base to reach the beeswax. He now had to wait until the clay dried out so, hiding the model again, he went in search of items to repair. Speaking pleasantly to the people he met, he explained his presence in the settlement and his hope of work. Being a fine day in early Spring, most of the inhabitants were working in their fields below the fort, either weeding the winter-sown wheat, ploughing other areas with one or two oxen pulling the ards ready for the barley sowing, or tending sheep on the higher pastures. Kran saw that many of those animals had already been herded into the grassy areas between two of the outer-most earthworks of the camp. For lambing, he guessed, as many of the horned ewes were very plump. He saw, too, that their fleeces were already beginning to look ragged and untidy so the Spring moult was clearly in progress. Climbing a higher bank, Kran saw that several women and children were indeed plucking wool from the sheep's backs and placing it in large baskets of woven willow. Some were using wood or bone combs to make it easier to pull off the wool. Separated from the ewe pens were other enclosures where the rams and older ewes were also being stripped. Spring was certainly a busy time but the hillfort seemed well organized and prosperous.

From his viewpoint on the bank, Kran looked down on the surrounding countryside, realizing that individual farmsteads appeared to run down hill, each ending at either a small brook or, on the other side of the enclosure, a larger river. In those well-watered lower fields there were many cattle, for there the pasture was more lush. Dividing all the fields were banks to keep animals within bounds and out of the ploughlands and growing crops. The whole area seemed well-populated and Kran marvelled at the obvious prosperity. It was no wonder people from other hillforts had moved here. If he could, he would stay himself. There was probably work enough and he would like to settle down, even taking a wife and raising his own family.

After a time he returned to where his tools were hidden beneath the storage hut, and was pleased to find the clay that covered his model was now dry. He made a good fire and baked the piece in its embers. As the clay heated, so the beeswax at its centre began to melt and run from the hole he had made. When this had all dripped out into a bowl he set it aside for the wax to harden for re-use, and put some of the scraps and filings of bronze from his small store into another pot. This pottery crucible he placed in the centre of the fire and heated it to a high temperature so the bronze became molten. Then, with infinite care, he poured it into the now hollow mould in place of the beeswax. While he was propping this up to cool and set he became aware of a young woman beside him.

"What are you making?" she asked. "You aren't Tollith the ironworker. I've not seen you before."

"I am Kran, a bronzeworker. This is my first day here and I am making a gift for your king."

"I am Alva. My family lives below this fort where my father, his brothers, my greatparents and all their children have a farm. We pay a tithe from our produce to the Chief in exchange for our land and his protection. But if I marry Tollith I will be superior to my own brothers and sisters because he is a craftsman."

Kran looked at her sharply and, seeing she was pleasing to the eye, determined then and there to marry her himself. He was a metalworker also and so was equal in status to Tollith as well as to all tribal teachers and poets. He was not an ordinary freeman. He was on a level with Tollith – and much younger.

"Who arranged this marriage?" he asked.

"Oh, Tollith, of course. Who else? My father agreed because he needs a new iron point to his ard share and thought to have it cheaper this way."

"I shall marry you myself," Kran declared. "Now I must continue with my work."

"And I with mine," Alva replied, taking her basket of sheep's wool to the adjacent hut and climbing its short ladder. When she emerged, having tipped the wool onto the pile already there, she said, "Tollith is a powerful man and he will fight you."

"No doubt," Kran shrugged, "and I shall win. I am a good fighter and fear no one."

When Alva had left, he examined his clay mould again and saw the bronze was not yet set. He decided to meet the remainder of the settlement's people to seek work, and so moved from roundhouse to roundhouse, explaining his craftsmanship, and offering to repair broken pieces. In this way he was handed several small items which he took back to his fire. He saw at once that the precious mould was no longer there. His raven had gone! Bewildered, he looked about for a possible culprit but none was in sight.

He thought of Tollith. It had to be him! Jealousy, not only because he was no longer the only skilled craftsman in the settlement, but because he could have seen the conversation with Alva, his wife to be. Filled with an instant fury, Kran strode across the enclosure to the ironworker's small forge. When the smith saw him coming, he moved away from his hut and waited, hands on his hips.

"So, bronzeman, what do you want?"

"My mould! You've taken it!"

"Taken your mould? Why would I do that?"

But the smile on Tollith's face was one of glee so Kran knew his suspicions were right. "I shall fight you," he cried. "I shall win it back by force unless you give it to me now. I am a powerful fighter! A winner of battles! A conqueror in single combat!"

Tollith's response was to swing his arm as if to knock Kran down. When the younger man ducked, the other arm came at him and knocked him off balance. Winded, Kran paused a moment and then hooked one foot behind the other's knees in an attempt to fell him. The only result was that he himself landed on the ground and had to suffer the indignity of hearing Tollith laugh. Furious, he regained his feet and fought back, but the bigger man outreached him every time and his own blows fell ineffectually on the forearms.

"So, mighty fighter, winner of battles, what now?"

"What now?" replied Kran. "I'll take Alva from you and marry her myself!" He then spat in the face of Tollith and retreated hastily, knowing he had delivered the ultimate insult.

Still furious but unsure of his future strategy, he returned to where he had left his tools. They were still there but the mould had not been returned. He gathered all his belongings together, kicked earth onto the remains of the fire and marched off towards the main east gate. A wild idea then came into his head. He would seize a bagful of the small round pebbles that were piled on the parapet. They were sling shot for use in time of attack, and he was adept at using them. Having lived on the edge of the Great Sea to which raiders sometimes came, most of the boys and young men had been taught to use the sling. If he took some of the shot he could make a sling – it needed only a piece of leather and two lengths of thin cord. He had been particularly accurate with a horizontal throw, rather than the overarm, and it would be deadly enough to fell Tollith. But he would have to take the pebbles later for there were a couple of men nearby who were watching him, so he strode down the hill to the first of the farmsteads. There he enquired where he would find the father of Alva and was pointed to a ploughed field a short distance away. A man was leading two yoked oxen and these dragged a heavy log over the earth so as to cover the newly sown seed. When Kran shouted to him, he pulled the animals to a halt and waited. He had the typically twisted and misshapen body of a farmer – his left shoulder permanently raised from the downward pressure of his right arm on the handle of the ard when ploughing, and his legs somewhat bandy from long standing with feet apart and back bent when reaping with a sickle. His face was cheerful, though, and his smile friendly.

When the greetings were over, Kran explained that he wished to marry Alva and was prepared to equal Tollith in the gift of goods, whatever the dowry her father gave her. This, he suspected, would be a cow in calf, whereas he would pay in items of bronze, yet to be made.

"I am younger than Tollith, as you can see. I shall father many sons. With continuing favour from the king they shall become warriors, and then their sons rise to be great nobles. Tollith is ill-favoured and his daughters will be ugly, cursed by the gods and hard to marry off. Give her to me and your family will thrive."

The farmer eyed him up and down, rubbing his nose thoughtfully. "Ask the gods", he said finally. "The matter is in their hands. If you truly wish for Alva, make a sacrifice and have the priest read the omens. I will abide by that. Now I must continue my work, otherwise the rooks will take the unburied seed."

Returning to the settlement, Kran sought out the priest and found him near the shrines in the centre of the enclosure. He was filling a deep pit from a nearby pile of earth. Without speaking, Kran took up another wooden shovel, its edges encased in iron for protection, and helped with the labour. After a while the priest paused for breath and Kran enquired what this pit had been for.

"It held the last of the seedcorn," he was told. "The gods of the Earth and the Underworld have been kind to us this year – the seed had not become mouldy over the winter months in its dark hole and has germinated well when sown. The family who owned this pit has fields that are now sprouting green and they have made a thank offering to the gods. They gave a sheep for sacrificial slaughter and I have just laid the body on the floor of this hole. Now we fill it in. When Autumn comes they will dig another pit for the new harvest's seed."

They took up the shovels again and completed their task. Then Kran spoke humbly to the priest and explained he wished to marry Alva but that she was spoken for by another. "If I give the gods an offering of my bronzework perhaps they will help me. And if I sacrifice a cock and you find omens in its entrails that give me divine approval, then her father will also aid me. For this I will make you a bronze pin for your cloak."

The priest looked at him shrewdly. "You are the bronzesmith newly come, and I hear that already there is enmity between you and Tollith. Do your offerings also carry the wish to do him harm? Not only to win from him the girl but to cause him damage in other ways?"

Kran remembered his thoughts about the slingshot and Tollith's death. Hesitating a moment, he said, "No longer. Let the gods decide. I will hold to their decision."

Then he burst out, "But he did take the mould of a raven I was making to give to the Chief! I did wish him ill for that deed. The raven is the totem of my own family and so especially to be revered."

The priest nodded. "Bring me a cock at dawn tomorrow and I will tell you more."

Kran paid for the cock with a bronze ring from his leather bag and took it to the priest at first light. The bird's throat was cut with a ceremonial knife and the blood allowed to drip into a metal bowl. Feathers were then plucked from its belly and a slit made in the bare flesh. From this the entrails spilt onto the flattened earth and lay twisted and steaming in the cool air of dawn. Kran kept his distance but the priest crouched low over them, occasionally moving his position to gain a different aspect. Then he stood up, smiling.

"The gods are with you! You will gain the girl and that which is lost will be returned. But only if anger leaves your heart. Peace must prevail in the settlement."

Gratefully Kran agreed, although distressed that his hatred of Tollith had to be overcome. How to do this he did not know. The man still held his raven.

It was later in the day that he saw the ironsmith staring at him. Then Tollith strode across, anger on his face. "You have ill-wished me! I saw you with the priest and heard him mumbling his incantations and curses. Now my work is suffering and goes awry. The gods will no longer favour me. So take the girl! Alva is only of farming stock and I can find better."

"And the mould?" Kran demanded quickly. "The gods have been told of the theft. Would you want further harm to come to you? Give it back to me and all will be well."

After a moment Tollith put his hand within his tunic and pulled out the model. "Have it back, then! Your skill will never equal mine nor the favour of the chief be as great. Take it!"

With that he threw it viciously onto the cobbled pathway and turned away. Alarmed by the shattering of the clay, Kran snatched it up. He found the mould broken open but revealing a perfect bronze raven. Joyfully he rubbed away the dust and found it undamaged. The gods had truly been kind.

Later, from his bag of tools he took out his finest chisel. Carefully he added lines to the body of the bird to represent feathers and then, after a polish on his clothing, he felt satisfied. There was a sheen to the model that would please both the king and the deities. Then he went in search of Alva to show her what he had made. Later he would present the gift to the chief as he had promised.

From now on, life would be very good.

Based on:

"Iron Age Britain" by Barry Cunliffe. Batsford/English Heritage, 1997.

"Danebury" by Barry Cunliffe. Batsford/English Heritage, 1993.

"Wessex to A.D.1000" by Barry Cunliffe. Longman, 1997.

"Iron-Age Farm: The Butser Experience" by Peter J. Reynolds. British Museum Publications, 1979.

"Britain and the Celtic Iron Age" by Simon James & Valerie Rigby. British Museum Press, 1997.

"Discovering Prehistoric England" edited by James Dyer. Shire Publications, 1993.

"Danebury: The Story of an Iron Age Hillfort" by Barry Cunliffe. Danebury Trust, undated.

Leaflets and exhibits in *The Museum of the Iron Age,* Andover. Danebury Trust & Hampshire County Council

Chapter Three

Hayling Island, 98 A.D.

Foidran was old and had difficulty climbing into the ferry boat. Crossing the water to the island he was relieved to see the country ahead was nearly flat for hills and broken ground left him short of breath and shaky on his feet.

He paid the ferryman with a coin from the small hoard in his leather purse, hoping he had not misjudged its value. Nowadays it was difficult to see whose head was on the metal – sometimes, when his eyes were hazy, he saw two heads and became confused.

Once he had been a great man in his tribe. A singer, a bard, welcome at the feastings of his people for whom he would sing of great exploits and tales of splendid heroes. When age began to fail his voice, those at the back of the lord's hall could not hear him. His memory began to weaken also, and the names of places where great battles had been fought would leave his mind. He knew them well, of course, but could not recall them when needed. So his tribe found a younger singer, one who knew about more recent battles, tribe against tribe, his own Durotriges against the Dobunni, Belgae or the Atrebates. He had often thought that if all these British peoples had joined together in one great army they might have repelled the Romans. A few more leaders like Boudicca and Caratacus had been needed. Instead, the Britons had fought amongst themselves, settling old scores or greedily trying to increase their estates or kingdoms. Inevitably this had led some tribes to side with the invaders in the hope of gaining an advantage. Such a scheme had worked well, too. It was said that Cogidubnus, who had ruled among the Regni, had been allied with the Romans to his great gain, being made a Roman citizen by the Emperor Claudius and allowed to live in his great palace near Noviomagus and even rule over other peoples. In the end, of course, all this southern part of Britain had fallen under Roman influence and life was not the same.

His own home in the once prosperous port of Hengistbury, far to the west, was not the same, either. Fewer and fewer ships had come from Armorica across the sea, and even the previously thriving coastal trade had fallen away. The settlement had finally foundered and most of the inhabitants had left. Few traders used Hengistbury now. He knew the reason. The Romans, having conquered Gaul over the sea, had built themselves great roads for their merchandise and armies that led to more northern ports than those in Armorica. He had heard that Londinium was now the great trading city, but where that was he did not know. All he knew was that he needed somewhere to live until the gods took back his life in death.

When he had clambered from the ferry, he followed the trackway leading south and into the centre of the island. It did not matter where he went but he had been told there was a holy site there. Perhaps it would give him sanctuary. There might even be a priest. No druids, though, for they had been cruelly suppressed by the Romans who knew them to be the great spiritual leaders of the Britons and thus able to stir up resistance to the invasion. After the terrible battle on the Island of Mona, far away to the north west, druids had had to live in secret and were few. Priests were allowed to remain, however, for they served gods very similar to those of the Romans and there was no hostility. So there might be a priest here.

By asking his way, Foidran came to a woodland clearing. There he saw not only a circular sanctuary but a gang of workmen building a stone wall, square in shape, to surround the courtyard.

In his quavering voice he called out, "Greetings! May the gods be with you!"

The men straightened up and turned towards him. "Greetings!" they replied, but said no more. He was, after all, a stranger.

"A priest?" he asked. "Is there one here?"

"I am the priest," was the reply. "I am Dino. Do you need me? Have you a sacrifice to make? And to which God?"

"No, no. I am but a traveller, looking for a people in need of a bard."

"Ah!" Dino released his tunic which he had tucked into his belt while he worked. "That is another matter. Of whom do you sing?"

"I sing of the battle glory of warriors and heroes. Of great kings and noble princes. Of valorous deeds and protection by the holy ones."

"And your heroes? Of what tribe are they, for by your voice I do not think you come from hereabouts?"

"I am Foidran of the Durotriges, far to the west. I sing of men's bravery under attack, of the splendour of feasting halls, the glitter of their war gear, the beauty of the women – ."

"Yes, yes," Dino interrupted, "but we have not the same great ones. Here, in the southern lands of the Atrebates and the kingdom of the Regni, our heroes are other. Your songs would not interest us."

Foidran made no reply. Hope left him. He was truly a man doomed by the gods to wander, with no home and no wealth. He felt his shoulders sag and the smile leave his face. Unwanted. He was quite unwanted. He stared about him but saw nothing. Only death lay ahead.

Dino hesitated a moment and then shrugged. "I can at least feed you," he said. "The workmen here will have their midday break soon and you can join us. Let it not be said that a priest of this place turned away a supplicant who had come in peace, denying him a meal or a horn of mead to give him cheer."

Unexpectedly, tears filled the old eyes. "May the gods bring you blessings," he mumbled. "I am indeed suffering hunger. It is long since I ate, for I have few coins left."

He was led towards the enclosure and was encouraged to sit on the grass, his back against the new wall. In relief he relaxed and smiled his thanks both to Dino and to a workman who had given him a hand when he tried to lower himself to the

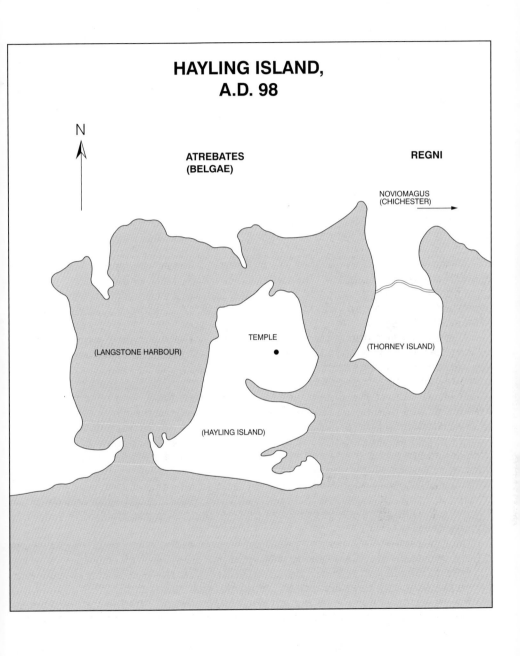

HAYLING ISLAND,
A.D. 98

N

ATREBATES
(BELGAE)

REGNI

NOVIOMAGUS
(CHICHESTER)

TEMPLE

(LANGSTONE HARBOUR)

(THORNEY ISLAND)

(HAYLING ISLAND)

ground. Here he was safe and about to be fed. The dark night would threaten him less with food in his belly and their kindness in his memory.

After the small meal was finished he asked about the sanctuary and to which gods the shrine was dedicated. Dino explained that the main god was Silvanus but that many others were worshipped. "We have a new figure of Silvanus, shaped in bronze and as a stag. He is very splendid."

"You mean you make figures of your gods?" Foidran asked in puzzlement. "But how can the spirits be captured? Surely they are free to roam where they will, throughout the skies and all the wide earth? I think your Silvanus must be a god of a very small locality, tied down to his bronze image." He looked at Dino but saw he was not pleased.

"Our gods are as powerful as ever," the priest declared crossly. "They roam wide and free. It is only in these latter years that we have learnt this figure-making from the Gauls. And they had learnt it from their conquerors, the Romans. So now we, too, like to have statues of our gods – they seem more real to the people. I think your priests are behind the times and foolish."

Worried that he had been discourteous, Foidran murmured. "Maybe, maybe. I am unlearned in these things. The idea is new to me, that is all, and I beg your pardon."

After a moment Dino decided to forgive him. "Come!" he said. "I will take you inside the holy enclosure and you can see the new building of the shrine. Until now it has been of timber, as you no doubt realize, but we are remaking it in stone in the Gaullish style. It is to be a temple and very rich. Even roofed in stone and with pillars all round."

A temple was a strange idea to Foidran. Mostly his own people worshipped the gods in the open air or round a small and house-like sanctuary. He could not see why, if the divine beings were everywhere, they needed a special kind of building, quite unlike the dwellings of the worshippers. And why did Gaul have to be copied by people in Britain? But then it was all change these days, with change following change. He was glad he was old and would not live much longer.

Remembering Dino's dislike of criticism, he murmured respectfully that this must be a rich settlement to be able to afford the stone. It would, after all, have to cross the water as he could see no signs of stone on the island, which was well-timbered. Perhaps Cogidubnus of Noviomagus had supplied the money – he had heard his palace was not far off. Guiltily he realized offerings of coin from visitors to the temple would be expected. So he felt again in his pouch for a coin and humbly handed it to Dino. "An offering to Silvanus," he said, "in gratitude for the welcome received here."

Having taken the money, the priest led him out of the enclosure. "I must return to work," he said. "May the gods go with you."

Feeling himself dismissed, Foidran walked back to the trackway and wandered disconsolately along its muddy path. When he was out of sight of the temple, he slowed his pace until finally he halted. What should he do now? His store of coins was nearly gone and he needed shelter for the night. Depressed again, he waited for inspiration. None came, so he resumed his wandering. After a few minutes he heard a call behind him. One of the temple workmen was running towards him, so he stopped and waited.

"Old man, Dino has sent me. There is a widow in the village who has three children and would be glad to give a traveller a bed for the night. Let me show you the way."

Foidran was guided to a group of huts and they halted outside one of them. "Bega!" the man called. "I have a traveller in need of shelter. Have you a spare skin on which he could sleep and a mouthful of gruel for his supper?"

A woman emerged from the hut, a baby to her breast. Her robe was torn and dirty, her hair matted and her feet bare. She looked closely at Foidran and then admitted she had both skins and food. When he had thanked the workman, Foidran followed Bega into the hut and saw at once it was in a poor state with holes in the thatched roof. The housedog snarled at him but he paid it no attention, being more intent on finding his way across the floor. In the back of the hut it was very dark so he shuffled his feet along, scared of falling over a child or some other object. Finally Bega told him he could sit down.

"I have little money," he told her apologetically. "Only a few coins now, and they were given to me by a kind wayfarer I met on the road."

She asked him how much he had. When he told her she sighed. "Not enough! Not enough! How can I feed you for that?"

The children came to him then, a boy of about four and a girl two years younger. They were both thin and although he could not see them well in the gloom, he sensed they were frail. After a while they clung to his legs and stared into his face. When they did not move away he became embarrassed and was at a loss for words. Not knowing what else to do, he began to sing. It was a quiet song, about the Lady of the Moon and was not of valiant deeds or bloody battles.

After a while he realized the children had fallen asleep, lying against his legs, their thumbs in their mouths.

When Bega saw them she brought the baby across to him. "Here," she said. "Take this one, too, then I can fetch the water without worry." Picking up an old leather bucket, she left the hut, only returning from the stream when it was full. As the children still slept she began to prepare the evening meal of gruel and flat bread, which she baked on the hearth stones. Gradually her actions became slower and slower until she was still. "If you were to guard the children all day and sing them to sleep, I could go to work in the fields. I would not then charge you for the food. Could you do this? Since my husband died of sickness, I and the children have near enough starved. It seems that we, like you, need help to live."

Foidran replied, "I would be honoured to do this for you. And grateful. My old bones could not walk much more."

So it was arranged. During the day he occupied the older children with hunts for fuel and little games and, when daylight faded, sang them to sleep. Bega took the infant to the fields with her, wrapped in a shawl tied across her back, and earned a little food: a fish, a bowl of ewe's milk or an egg or two. Once, when she had been out all day, she returned with a lump of sheep's cheese and a vessel filled with good rye flour. That night they feasted. She seemed less anxious now, while Foidran knew a peace he had not known for a long time.

When darkness fell it became his habit to leave the hut and, under the quiet sky and the stars, to thank the gods for their goodness to him. He had no need to go back to the temple with its formal surroundings, for the gods were all about him –

above, below and on every side. Their spirits were in the trees, the streams, the daytime birds, the sheep, Bega, the children and even the mangy housedog.

Then he would sigh, knowing himself content. The gods had not deserted him, after all.

Based on:

"Internal Organisation and Deposition at the Iron Age Temple on Hayling Island" by Anthony King & Graham Soffe. Proceedings of the Hampshire Field Club and Archeological Society, Vol. 53, 1998.

"Iron Age Britain" by Barry Cunliffe. Batsford/English Heritage, 1997.

"Roman Britain" by Martin Millett. Batsford/English Heritage, 1995.

"Romans in Britain" by Rodney Legg. Heinemann, 1983.

"Rome against Caratacus" by Graham Webster. B. T. Batsford, 1981.

"Roman Britain: Outpost of the Empire" by H. H. Scullard. Thames & Hudson, 1994.

"Shrines & Sacrifice" by Ann Woodward. Batsford/English Heritage, 1992.

"The Gods of Roman Britain" by Miranda J. Green. Shire Archaeology, 1983.

Ordnance Survey reference of the Temple site (on private land): SU 724 029

Chapter Four

Silchester, 296 A.D.
(Calleva Atrebatum)

Lydia listened to her husband arguing with Marcellus in the dining room. Naturally the subject would be politics – nothing much else was talked about these days.

Not wishing to miss the conversation, she took from the servant the tray with the wine ewer and goblets of pale green glass. Pushing aside the curtain that hung over the doorway she entered quietly, placed the tray on a low table and, having filled each goblet, took them to the men.

Marcellus was lying on a couch, his long legs dangling over the edge. "There you are wrong, Didos," he was saying. "This Allectus is a nobody. He was only a treasury official, after all. What does he know about governing? It's high time we had the Emperor in charge again."

Didos smiled his thanks to his wife before sipping the wine. He was a good husband: responsible, faithful, diligent at his work, fond of her. She did wish, however, that he was more attractive, for he was short, his neck too thick and his hands white and flabby. But, being dutiful herself, she smiled in return as a good wife should, and sat beside him on a stool.

"Ah, Lydia!", Marcellus said, waving his goblet in greeting to her. "How do you feel about Allectus, our newest ruler? I can't persuade Didos that he's a misfortune for Britain. He would have done better to have left us Carausius as governor – he at least had some character – instead of assassinating him."

"Carausius was nothing but a rogue, and you know it!" Didos broke in heatedly. "A usurper! If Emperor Diocletian had not been so busy in Rome he'd never have let such a thing happen. Carausius was due to be executed, don't forget! Allectus merely carried out that order."

"True! True!" Marcellus smiled. "And I suppose that makes Allectus a good ruler? I really can't see why. After all, he also usurped the rule, which is why we are stuck with him now. Are you in favour of that?" He twirled the wine glass and looked inquiringly at Didos, eyebrows raised.

Lydia could see her husband was being teased and was not taking it well. Marcellus was so much more sophisticated, his thinking clearer, his mind more alert. He was also younger and better looking and she saw that Didos would soon be humiliated. Rather than listen further, she rose, replenished the men's glasses and left the room. In the privacy of the herb garden she sat on a bench to enjoy the sunshine. Why did men have to argue all the time, especially when politics could raise tempers more quickly than any other subject? But the question Marcellus had asked her? How did she really feel about Allectus?

She thought first about the man he had assassinated, Carausius, the self-styled ruler of Britain. He had been a clever and resourceful man, even if as dishonest as Didos had said. He had come originally from Gallia Belgica, on the other side of the Narrow Sea, and had been placed in command of the Roman fleet with its headquarters at Boulogne. His task had been to guard both shipping and coastal settlements against barbarian pirates and raiders. Smiling, she remembered the audacity of the man and how he would allow the fierce Franks and Saxons to raid at will along the two coasts, delaying their capture until they had filled their ships with booty. Then he would attack, remove their loot to his own ships, keeping the bulk of it for himself but distributing the rest among his seamen. No wonder he was popular!

It had been when the Emperor had heard of this abuse of command that he had ordered the death of Carausius. But he (very sensibly, Lydia thought) had taken refuge in Britain and set himself up as sole ruler, naming himself "Restitutor Britanniae" and turned the country into an independent province. He had ruled for seven years and she could remember no real dissent among the people, for he had ruled well. His control of the army was effective and the economy thrived, especially after he had minted large quantities of his own coinage which spread his name throughout the land. He had even indulged in self-agrandisment to the extent of declaring he was equal in status to Diocletian and thus also an emperor of the Roman empire.

Lydia smiled again. The man had been a traitor to Rome and very corrupt but she could not help but admire him. He had been so forceful. And, it had to be said, the pirate raiders had indeed been prevented from invading Britain in depth. Perhaps this was because there were now forts along the south-eastern coasts as well as the new one at Portus Adurni, not far from Clausentum. The tide had turned for Carausius though, when the imperial army under Constantius captured the vital port of Boulogne. It was then that Carausius was assassinated by his own finance minister, Allectus, who in his turn, became the self-appointed ruler of Britain.

It was about this man Allectus that Lydia's husband and Marcellus were arguing so fruitlessly in the dining room. Sighing, she re-entered the house to see if they wished for more wine. She liked her house. As she passed from the sunshine to the long, open corridor that ran the length of the new wing where the best rooms were, she admired the extensions. Last year, when Didos had been promoted to member-ship of the Ordo, that important group of citizens which was the town council, he had decided to enlarge the house. Such a promotion was based on property qualifications and these, because of his extensive land holdings outside the town, he had been able to fulfil. In addition, as a wealthy man, he had made a considerable contribution towards the new town walls and for statues to embellish the forum. He was, therefore, eminently suitable to join the Ordo.

Both he and Lydia were pleased with his election and now she looked forward to entertaining more elevated people than before. Calleva was, after all, an important

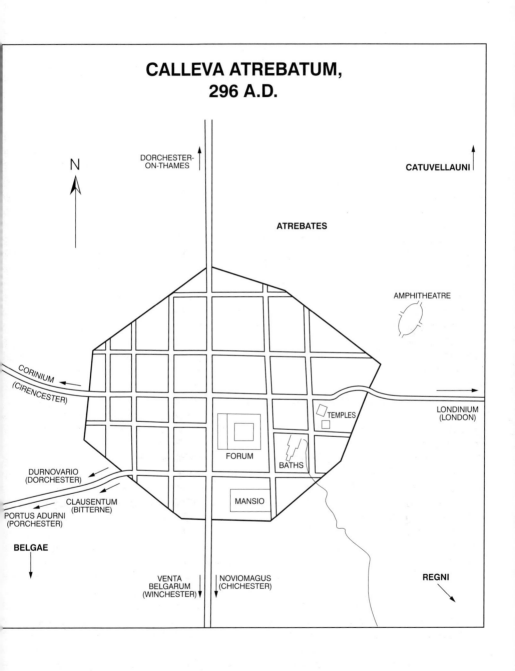

CALLEVA ATREBATUM, 296 A.D.

N

DORCHESTER-ON-THAMES

CATUVELLAUNI

ATREBATES

AMPHITHEATRE

CORINIUM (CIRENCESTER)

LONDINIUM (LONDON)

TEMPLES

FORUM

BATHS

DURNOVARIO (DORCHESTER)

CLAUSENTUM (BITTERNE)

PORTUS ADURNI (PORCHESTER)

MANSIO

BELGAE

VENTA BELGARUM (WINCHESTER)

NOVIOMAGUS (CHICHESTER)

REGNI

town, the regional capital – the civitas – of the tribal lands of the Atrebates, and with Venta Belgarum, Durnovario and Noviomagus Regnensium, was one of the most flourishing in southern Britain. Moreover, the town stood at the centre of an important road system, upgraded by the Romans from the original native trackways. This meant that officials, army officers and those using the imperial postal system passed through, some resting at the 'mansio' with its many small rooms for overnight accommodation, while others welcomed a stay in a well-appointed private house such as hers. The town was really a major staging post for central Britain, gaining financially from this, and Lydia recognised the wisdom of Didos' investment in enlarging their property.

Later that day they both went to the forum for their usual evening stroll. Her marketing had been done in the morning with a slave, and now there were few traders left in the covered walkways that lay round three sides of the square. The central, open part was filled with those such as themselves who had come to gossip to their friends and to see and be seen by others. Calleva was a proud city, having been here before the Romans came, and both Lydia and Didos were pleased to be able to trace back their ancestry to the elite of the Atrebates tribe of the Britons. Now, being elevated to the Ordo, they were more important still.

After a while, Didos turned to his wife. "Come with me to the basilica," he said. "I would like you to meet a newly arrived member of the judiciary, Aurelius Plautius. I believe we'll find him in the law court or else the council chamber."

Inside, a man of middle-age came forward to greet them. While the introductions were being made, Lydia thought the newcomer was very tense. Didos must also have seen this for he suggested quietly that she should return to the forum to rejoin her friends. As she left to do so, she heard Plautius say, "He has sailed! The ships seem to be heading for Clausentium. What will happen when they land I do not know! May the gods protect us because –" and then he lowered his voice and she heard no more.

She wondered what that was about and became increasingly puzzled when other members of the Ordo hurried passed her to join Didos and the magistrate. Clearly an emergency of some sort, but what? A war? Revolt? And who was 'he'? The Emperor?

Across the open space of the forum she saw Marcellus in serious conversation with another man. As he had so recently been in her home, she did not hesitate to walk up to them. "Gentleman, I beg your pardon for this intrusion, but I am anxious to know why so many of the councillors are hurrying to the basilica. Is there trouble?" Neither man answered her so she hazarded a guess. "Is it Allectus?"

"Certainly it is!" Marcellus replied. "I knew that upstart ruler would bring us trouble! I told Didos he would. And now I'm proved right. He's no more the real ruler of Britain than I am and I don't wonder the Emperor –"

Then he paused, gazing speculatively at Lydia. Placing a hand on her arm he said gently. "I should run along, my dear, if I were you. This is men's talk."

Inwardly furious, she moved off to join her female friends, many of whom were watching the basilica with worried faces. "Aula!" she cried, hurrying to another woman. "What is happening? Is there a revolt? A war with the Catuvellauni, perhaps?"

"I don't know, either," Aula replied. "But it's serious. Very serious." Nervously she pulled at the end of the shawl that covered a shoulder. "Very serious!" she repeated. "And my daughter has just given birth to a boy. Her firstborn. She lives south of here, you see, near the highway to Venta, in a small villa. Just a farmstead, really, with no defences at all. I just hope her soldier husband is at home – but then he's only an auxiliary and not even a centurion. He's quite young, so he's not a Roman citizen yet – he's a long way off his twenty-five years in the army – so he won't have any influence at all. Oh, dear! My poor girl!"

Tears began to roll down her cheeks so Lydia put an arm round her. "Come, Aula! You talk as if we're being attacked! We don't even know if there's an emergency yet!"

"But we do!" the other woman cried. "I had a terrible dream last night and there were men everywhere – killing and stabbing and murdering little children. My dreams are always right, so it's war! It's war! Oh, dear!"

After a while Lydia passed her over to the female slave who led her away, still weeping. She had become nervous herself now. She had seen that the men had been deeply concerned, very serious, and yet agitated. Could it be war? Something to do with both the Emperor and Allectus? If the Emperor was attacking Britain in order to depose Allectus, then truly it was war. She looked round the forum. The few remaining traders were unpatronised, packing up their goods to return to their homes in the suburbs, for nobody was still interested in buying. Most people were silent, just staring at the doorway of the basilica, waiting for the men to emerge. At last, in small groups, the councillors appeared. From among them Plautius, as senior magistrate, came to the front and held up his arms for silence. At once all talking ceased.

"Citizens of Calleva Atrebatum," he called. "We are in danger. The Emperor Diocletian is coming to take this province of Britain back to Roman rule. Our leader, Allectus and his army will be attacked. This means war. You have to decide on which side you stand – that of the Emperor or that of Allectus. Although no army is in our area, we have received messages that a great fleet of ships has been sighted off the south coast. We believe it is making for the fort there, built by our previous ruler, Carausius. Moreover, we have heard that the Emperor Diocletian has declared that Constantius, his deputy, is now governor of Gaul. This man is amassing a fleet and army in the River Seine and is threatening to invade Britain by way of the River Thamesis and the town of Londinium. So we are in a perilous state, with two armies about to be ranged against us with attacks from both south and east. I suggest you all return to your homes and at night barricade yourselves in, for we do not know what the next day will bring. Gather your weapons so that you may fight if needs be, on one side or the other, and if you have treasures, bury them. So go now, and may the gods protect us all."

When the speech was ended, everyone began to talk at once. Lydia pushed through the crowd to find Didos who was still among the members of the Ordo on the steps of the basilica. When she found him he was very distressed. He had seen Allectus as a great hero, a splendid ruler and now he was made out to be no more than a usurper on the run.

The two returned home and told their household of the situation, then following the magistrate's suggestion, they gathered together their most precious pieces of gold, silver, pewter and bronze. These they placed in a wooden box and waited for nightfall before burying it in the orchard, out of sight of the servants.

After the digging, Lydia was concerned to see that Didos was physically distressed, short of breath and with a high colour. She helped him into the house and brought him a glass of wine. "Drink this," she urged, "then lie on the couch. You aren't accustomed to physical work, after all. You'll feel better after a rest."

She sat beside him until he fell asleep and then wandered out into the garden. She did not want to leave all this if war came close. Her new roses smelled wonderful. It was strange to think there had been none in Britain until the Romans had brought them. They were, after all, a very civilizing people, despite an innate arrogance. And now – what now? War, was it? Allectus against Constantius and the Emperor? For the first time she regretted that the town of Calleva stood at the junction of so many major highways, for an army was bound to arrive here some day soon. In war it did not really matter whose army it was, for inevitably there would be killings and lootings, house-burnings and destruction.

Gradually, the days and nights passed but with no sign of war. News did come through to the Ordo, though, brought by messengers on horseback, and with Didos somewhat recovered and frequently at the basilica, Lydia was able to keep abreast of the situation. She heard that an invading army had evaded the garrison and ships attached to Portus Adurni, Allectus' fort on the coast, and had landed somewhere not far from Clausentum. A sea fog had arisen and hidden the two navies from each other, enabling the invaders to land unopposed. After burning their boats on the sea's edge, they had begun their northward march towards Venta before aiming for Londinium. Lydia feared for Aula's daughter and the baby son but there was nothing she could do except try to console her distraught friend.

Two days later came news that the second army of the Imperial forces, led by Constantius himself, had earlier created an effective diversion in the Narrow Sea to draw off troops and ships from the more westerly attack. Sailing up the River Thamesis they had captured Londinium before any of Allectus' troops could arrive to burn it down as a defensive measure. Those in Calleva became increasingly frightened, with Didos again suffering a collapse. Few people now spent time in the public baths, and fewer still went to entertainments in the amphitheatre although many more than usual went to the temple. Most of the traders had left the forum, preferring seclusion in the countryside, and only the produce sellers remained. With her husband increasingly feeble Lydia felt very much alone, as many of their friends had deserted the town. Aula fled, too, but to where Lydia did not know. Even Marcellus was absent.

As the days went by it became clear that two opinions were forming among those remaining in the town. Some citizens were prepared to back Allectus and fight for him, while others felt a greater safety lay with the Emperor Diocletian and the invading deputy Constantius. Two parties thus developed and social tensions were high. No one knew who sided with whom so suspicion and fear were prevalent. There was little entertaining now and on some days the forum was so deserted that none of the country folk or those from the suburbs came to trade. Lydia guessed that they, too, were hiding goods and storing foodstuffs against the coming war.

Idling one day in the garden, Lydia heard a subdued cry from a nearby shed. Full of fear, she called, "Who's there?"

From inside came a voice she recognized as that of Marcellus. "Help me, Lydia! Please help me – I am wounded."

Quickly she pulled open the door and saw him propped against a far wall, blood on his breastplate and a wound to his neck. "I went to fight for the Emperor," he said, "but some of Allectus' men caught me during their retreat. I need water. Please help me."

Without speaking, Lydia withdrew and, as casually as she could entered the house. Didos must not know an enemy of Allectus was on the property. Seeing a servant, she sent him for a jug of cold water and a glass. While waiting for them, she went in search of cloth with which to bind up the wound and pulled off the cover of a small couch. When the servant returned she told him to put the tray on the garden table. Strolling after him, she waited until he had gone, then went across to the hut. Marcellus was clearly apprehensive on her return, and she realized that, for all he knew, she might also be on the side of Allectus – as he knew was Didos – and might bring armed men to capture him. When he had drunk sufficient of the water, she used the gardener's pruning knife to cut and tear the cloth. Soaking a piece in the water jug, she bathed the wound, which was still bleeding a little, placed a pad over the cut and bandaged his neck.

"There!" she said. "You'll be alright now. But don't move more than you must."

Marcellus caught her hand. "May the gods bless you, Lydia. I thought I would bleed to death." He closed his eyes and lay back again. "The battle's not far off, you see," he murmured. "I never even got through to the Imperial army coming up from the coast. Allectus was in the way. He was retreating and his men found me in a wood. I managed to wound one of them before I was hit myself by a sword blow. I think they left me for dead but when night came I managed to cover the few miles here to Calleva." He smiled briefly. "Your side gate was unlatched, Lydia, so I just crawled in. I couldn't have reached my own house!"

"I thank the gods you're safe!" she exclaimed.

He caught her hand again and asked anxiously "Does Didos know I'm here? Have you told anyone?"

"No, no! And Didos is ill. I shall not tell him."

As he did not release her hand, she sat on the hard earth beside him until he fell into a quiet sleep. When his fingers relaxed she took up the jug and glass and sauntered back to the house, leaving the tray on a table in the dining room. She thought she had better make sure that her husband was all right, not liking to leave him for too long and found he was up from his bed, staring from the window.

"What were you doing?" he demanded. "Having a servant take water to the garden but returning it yourself with an empty jug? Why, Lydia? Had the gardener not watered the plants?"

She laughed as easily as she could. "Just one rose had been omitted, so I gave it a drink. That is all."

"But it's not all, you know. You have blood on your dress. Whose? What are you up to?"

She did not know how to answer and so told the truth. "Marcellus," she said. "He was wounded in a battle near here and needed water. So I took him some."

"That man! And who was he fighting? Allectus, I swear by the gods! A traitor! I won't have him on my property! I tell you Lydia, I won't harbour traitors! Allectus is our ruler!"

To her alarm, he struggled to put his cloak round his shoulders and set off for the dining room and the garden door. At that moment a servant ran in.

"Master! Master! News has come! Allectus has been killed in battle! Constantius and the Emperor have won!"

"No!" shouted Didos. "No! I won't believe it. Allectus was a good ruler. He can't be dead! And to think my wife sided with the enemy! Leave me! Leave me! Go, Lydia, you are not wanted in this –." Then clutching his chest he staggered to a couch.

In alarm, Lydia and the servant ran to him but his eyes were open and no breath came. "He is dead, Madam. May the gods receive his spirit. His heart, I think, was bad."

Dazed, Lydia closed her husband's eyes and wept. He had been good to her and there was great affection between them. She mourned his passing in genuine sorrow. After a while she told the servant to see that his master was laid on his bed and that the women were sent for. It was only later that she thought of the battle and remembered Marcellus. Slowly she walked to the garden and made her way to the shed.

"Didos has died," she said sombrely. "His heart failed. And news has come that Allectus has been killed. So the Emperor rules us again." Then she added sadly, "I don't think Didos could stand the death of his hero." She did not reveal that he knew of the wounded man in the garden and that it was partly this information that had struck him down. She would keep that to herself.

"Come," she said. "Now you can enter my home and be cared for properly." Smiling a little, she added wryly. "This shed isn't the best place to nurse you."

With her help, Marcellus managed to regain his feet, and the two of them passed slowly through the garden and into the house.

Based on:

"Calleva Atrebatum: A Guide to the Roman Town at Silchester." Calleva Museum, 1995.

"Roman Towns in Britain" by Guy de la Bédoyère. Batsford/English Heritage. 1992.

"Roman Britain" by T. W. Potter. British Museum, 1983.

"Romans in Britain" by Rodney Legg. William Heinemann, 1983.

"Roman Britain: Outpost of the Empire" by H. H. Scullard. Thames & Hudson, 1994.

"Wessex to AD 1000" by Barry Cunliffe. Longman, 1997.

"Roman Britain" by Martin Millett. Batsford/English Heritage, 1995.

Displays & Exhibits on Calleva Atrebatum (Silchester) at Reading Museum.

Displays in the Site Museum at Silchester.

Chapter Five

Winchester, A.D. 964

"I wouldn't mind as much," Leofric the priest told his wife, "if Bishop Ethelwold was not so rich – well, not him, exactly, but his huge diocese. It seems to get bigger and richer by the year." He could see that Edfrith was debating whether to stay and listen to his grumbles or retire to another chamber. To forestall her departure he added, "You may be tired of what I have to say, but I am weary of the situation. Remember that, wife."

Resignedly Edfrith settled herself again and, picking up her distaff, began to spin. "I do remember, my lord, that life has become unjust. And I mourn it. The recompense was not enough for the loss of your fine house at Chilcombe nor for our dwelling that lay in the grounds of Nunnaminster. I do know that, and I truly sorrow for you – and for our family, too."

"Where else," Leofric questioned angrily, "will I gain a priestly position of such quality and prestige? To be one of the chaplains to the holy ladies of the Nunnery was an honour. Now I am discarded and will have to seek employment elsewhere. This new fashion for priests to live like celibate monks will do the Church no good."

"I know," she soothed. "But Bishop Ethelwold will find you other work, I'm sure. After all, he was born here and must know everyone, so he could place you as a chaplain to a rich merchant. Unless you wish to follow the Bishop's wishes and dis-avow your wife and children? And then become a celibate priest or monk yourself?"

He made a gesture of dismissal. "Of course not! How could I? I love the children and besides, I am used to the married state. Celibacy would not be to my liking. Even the King, who has put aside his own wife, has only done so to wed another so he does not favour celibacy, either."

They both relapsed into silence but he was still angry. Everything had been so satisfactory before Ethelwold had become bishop here. But the blame for that, he supposed, lay with King Edgar for appointing him. Too many of his bishops were celibate monks – Oswald at Worcester, for instance, and even Dunstan, the archbishop of Canterbury. That they were holy, devout and zealous he did not doubt but the Church was being changed. Perhaps the enthusiasm of the king for all things monkish and this new revival of monasticism was due to his education at Ethelwold's Benedictine abbey of Abingdon on the Thames. But whatever the reason, many priestly careers were in ruins. Even his own property with its lands at Chilcombe was now under Ethelwold's jurisdiction and lordship, King Edgar having decreed that all properties within a seven mile radius of Winchester should go to the Bishop. At the same time he had returned to Ethelwold the royal lands at Alresford, at Downton in Wiltshire and Taunton in Somerset, and several other such manors. Too much land was being taken out of private hands and presented to the Church. It did not bode well for the future – when great thegns and aristocrats were deprived of their inheritances only resentment and bitterness could result. And all for what? For the further endowment of the New Minster and continuing rebuilding of the Old! And now there was the rebuilding of the Nunnery as well.

"Why did I not train as a lawyer?" Leofric exclaimed suddenly. "We'd have been all right then. I'd have had plenty of statutes, decrees and writs to draw up. Or a merchant in cloth? Nowadays clothiers are doing very well for themselves, what with the Church's ownership of so many of the sheep pastures hereabouts – including what used to be mine." He paused for a moment and then added, "Or a silversmith? With people so prosperous now – the Vikings not having attacked us since King Alfred's day – they're buying silver items again. Some, admittedly, as gifts for their churches, but much for their own gratification."

Edfrith looked up, smiling "I'm glad you did not choose to be a leather tanner! The area round Tanner Street and those little brooks smells awful! Being in Silver Street would have been much better."

He knew she was trying to ease his anger and frustration but her efforts only irritated him. He was justified in his annoyance. There were three Minsters in Winchester and now they were all under Benedictine rule – which, he had thought, was already an austere regime, so why all this extending and beautifying and the need for endowments? He could understand the need to do something about the Old Minster for it had been built over three hundred years ago as the cathedral of the diocese and was now too small. For this reason about sixty years ago the New Minster had been built for the townsfolk, immediately to the north, on land bought by the late King Edward the Elder, but placed so close to the Old Minster that when there was singing in both the sounds became confused. That was foolish, for a start. King Edward had also built the Nunnaminster on land given by his father, Alfred, to Queen Ealhswith, which lay just to the east of the other two Minsters. Now all three were being enclosed with walls and ditches and cut off from the life of the town. Even St. Swithun, in his burial place just outside the Old Minster could not keep things as they had been, for his tomb had now been incorporated in the new western extension. This was to keep the pilgrims in the dry, Leofric supposed, for the saint was now credited with many miracles and a dry and well-tended pilgrim donated more to the funds than a wet one. He knew he was being cynical but he was glad that Swithun had not been a monk – just a holy bishop.

Despite himself, Leofric was quite impressed by the New Minster, which was nearly double the size of the Old. That was said to have been built as a royal chapel as well as a cathedral, the royal palace being close by to the west and the bishop's dwelling just to its south. He had been told the New Minster was somewhat in the style found on the Continent, especially the proposed west tower which was said to carry echoes of Germany. In total, the ecclesiastical complex was very imposing and now quite large, reflecting the increasing wealth and status of the city and bishopric.

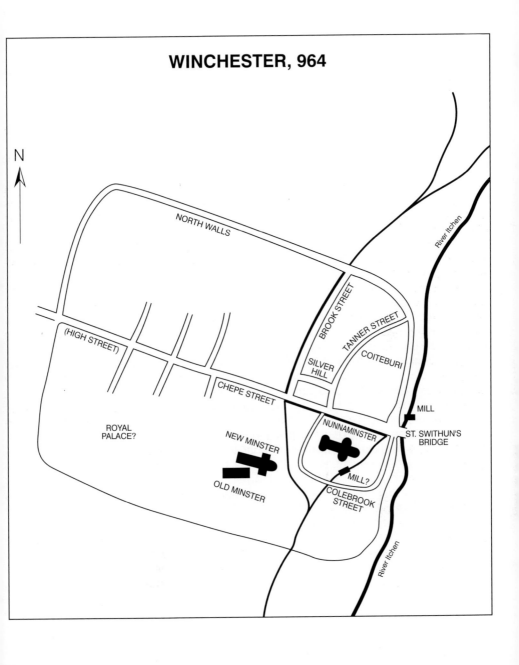

WINCHESTER, 964

N

NORTH WALLS

River Itchen

BROOK STREET

TANNER STREET

COITEBURI

(HIGH STREET)

SILVER
HILL

CHEPE STREET

MILL

ROYAL
PALACE?

NEW MINSTER

NUNNAMINSTER

ST. SWITHUN'S
BRIDGE

OLD MINSTER

MILL?

COLEBROOK
STREET

River Itchen

If he could have remained with the nuns, how happy he would have been! Now he could only watch as their abbey was rebuilt in stone, the original timber buildings having become somewhat derelict after the sixty or so years of use.

All the secular buildings were being removed, too – his own among them – so that the nuns could remain in quietness and solitude within their enclosure to pursue their Benedictine duties the better. New buildings, which would house those providing necessary lay services to the abbey, were being erected in a recently made area called Colebrook Street outside the nun's enclosure. Leofric felt sorry for those now isolated ladies, for they had previously been concerned with duties in the town as well as with religious matters. It would be a lonely life for them.

Nowadays Winchester was all bustle and noise, with builders everywhere and many carts rumbling along the streets bringing in stone from afar. Leofric sighed. "At least I'm not the only priest turned out," he remarked defensively. "All the married canons have gone from the two Minsters and many of them lost property, too. Even some of their houses have been knocked down to make way for Ethelwold's new boundary wall. We have been treated very badly, especially as the instruction to leave was so sudden and so unexpected. I'm becoming increasingly bitter about the situation and am losing my faith in the Christian charity of the Church itself. And all because Ethelwold wants celibate clergy."

Edfrith looked up from her spindle. "Hush, my lord!" she said urgently. "No one must hear you speak in such a manner or you'll never be given another appointment! Bear in mind at all times that the King, the Church and our Bishop rule our lives. Dissension causes only trouble for those who complain."

"I know, I know!" he replied, annoyance clear in his voice. "But what can I do now for money? Eh? How do we eat once the store of produce in my Chilcombe barns is used up, and my sheep and fat pigs have gone to the Bishop?"

In irritation he left the house and went towards the busy commercial part of the town. How did he find a household in need of a chaplain or a tutor for their young? How did he support his own family? He crossed the main market thoroughfare, Chepe Street, which ran from the west down to the river Itchen at St. Swithun's Bridge, wandering the streets in despair. Stopping outside the workshops of the various craftsmen, his gaze was drawn to the artefacts on display, and he regretted yet again that he had not been apprenticed to an artisan. He could have been happy making beautiful things. Instead, he had chosen the Church – and been betrayed. And only because he was married. He also had to bear the loss of his property in the Hundred of Chilcombe. It had, after all, been the security of his income from that property that had enabled him to offer for Edfrith in marriage. And now it was in the hands of Bishop Ethelwold. Life was bitter indeed.

Moving aimlessly down one of the cross lanes that led from Chepe Street, he saw ahead of him another priest. This man, Fremund, had been a canon of the New Minster and had also been dismissed for refusing to give up his married state. When they had greeted each other and Leofric was about to pour out his woes, Fremund laid a restraining hand on his arm.

"Do not despair, brother! Mayhap the bishop was right – our life as secular priests was too easy. We had not been tested enough in the ways of Our Lord. Now, when hardship has befallen us, is the time for trial of our faith."

He looked inquiringly at Leofric who only scowled. "I need bread for my children," he declared obstinately. "There are too many priests without positions since these changes. We will have to become tradesmen and in the ways of commerce I am ignorant. We shall starve."

"Be patient!" Fremund urged. "Cease to fill your soul with anger. What does anger achieve other than a fast-beating heart and raised colour in the cheek? No, Leofric, my friend. Be quiet in your mind – and of a good courage."

Impatiently Leofric turned away. He was in no mood for a sermon. Fremund might play the part of a saint if he wished but he was not willing to join him. Too many people were being seen as saints these days – Ethelwold among them. He walked on until he arrived near the river and the area known as Coiteburi, which had large and prosperous tenements and lay within the defences of the Burh. These walls had been created firstly by the authorities in Roman times and then rebuilt more recently by King Alfred. They defended the city against any further infiltration by the pagan Vikings who had attacked Winchester a hundred years ago and laid waste many of the richer churches. It was at that time of danger that many merchants had moved into the city for protection, creating the prosperous commercial centre it now was. In those hazardous days a new street had been made just within the northern walls to aid the defenders, and now Leofric followed it uphill. Along this northern road he passed a small glass foundry. Fascinated, he stopped to watch the men at work. He was told they were making small pieces in colour for a window of the new church of Nunnaminster. Blue, red, green and clear glass they were. Tiny pieces, later to be held together with strips of lead. Bitterness filled him again for he would not be there to see that window in place.

Thanking the glaziers for their patience with his questions, he moved on, too restless to stay. Passing other workshops and the fine timber tenements of their owners, he realised he had not been in this northern side of Chepe Street for some time. The town was growing and becoming a major trading centre. This was due he supposed, to the good road system, much of which still remained from the time of Rome, and to the river Itchen being partially navigable from the Solent. In addition, kings were both crowned and buried here and, with its ecclesiastical complex, was the chief city of the more northerly part of the shire, while Hamtun was the chief port to the south. It was after that town that the shire was named, although it had proved vulnerable to Viking raids. Leofric had been told it was a place full of foreigners and that the people were largely Jutish. He would not seek a new appointment there.

Turning down a side street, he came to the area where he knew the ironsmiths worked. Today he found the constant hammering of metal on metal too noisy to tolerate. He would be deaf in a week if he had to work here. What he needed was a new career that was carried out in a community, for he missed the company of his fellow priest at Nunnaminster as well as that of the nuns. Some of those ladies were very highborn indeed, as well as educated and intelligent. He hoped the rule of Saint Benedict would not distress them unduly, nor that the new austerity and seclusion would not prevent other widows or unmarried daughters from seeking security there. At least the new church would be beautiful, with glass in the windows and, no doubt, wonderful books.

Then he halted, startled by a thought. If Bishop Ethelwold had only the few unmarried Benedictine monks or priests working for him now, there might be a shortage of copyists with so many men having been dismissed. The scribes who had worked in the Minster scriptorium might all have gone and there be insufficient among the incomers from Abingdon Abbey to take their place. Could he do such work? Could he offer himself, for a wage, not to the bishop – for he would be averse to accepting a married priest – but to the abbess of the Nunnery as a copyist? After all, she knew him well.

Filled with excitement, he turned for home. In his neat hand he could write out Bishop Ethelwold's own translation into English of the "Regularis Concordia" of Saint Benedict, written for use in monasteries and nunneries. He had heard that the work had been undertaken at the request of King Edgar and his queen, and that Ethelwold had received an estate for his own use by way of thanks. Surely there must now be a shortage of copies – especially as it was rumoured there was to be a great council in the Old Minster to which the King would come with all the leading churchmen, abbots and abbesses, there to agree an acceptance of the rules expressed in Benedict's "Concordia". He could certainly copy that. Or if not that particular document, then he could translate the Psalms into English for the nuns. Or the religious poem, "An Admonition to Christian Living". Or a few chapters from Bede's "Life of Saint Cuthbert". The choices were many and all possible, for his understanding of Latin was good and his English tolerable.

As he neared his own house he had another thought. Why not write, in English, a life of Saint Edburga, who was actually buried in the Nunnery? As far as he knew, none had yet been written.

When he entered his hall he called for Edfrith. "Wife!" he shouted, "I have thought what to do!"

As he recounted his plans, she became more and more thoughtful. "My lord," she said finally, "the saints have spoken! Do you not remember that Saint Edburga was a royal princess, daughter of King Edward the Elder, and so aunt to our present king, Edgar? She spent nearly the whole of her life at Nunnaminster in that community of nuns and, for her holiness, is still revered by them. And King Edgar was once a pupil at Abingdon under Bishop Ethelwold, and it is they who are now urging the Benedictine rule to be imposed on the nuns. Everything links up, my lord! The Abbess is bound to agree and maybe you will again win favour with the bishop, despite being married!"

In delight they smiled at each other, deeply relieved that there was a chance of sorting out their futures.

Without more ado, Leofric gathered his writing equipment and soot-made ink and made a first draft of a letter to the Abbess. He reminded her of his present position as her dismissed chaplain and explained that he now wished to write a life of Saint Edburga. It would be in English, for the edification of her nuns and of the visiting pilgrims to the shrine. He emphasised the saint's royal connection and of how Bishop Ethelwold had insisted on treating the Saint's tomb with the greatest care when the old nunnery church had been dismantled. Now, as the Abbess would well know, miracles were being performed at Edburga'a grave and her fame had spread far and wide. He did no more than hint that this fame gave Nunnaminster great prestige and considerable income from the gifts of pilgrims, for she would know that well enough.

Both Leofric and Edfrith worked on this letter until they felt it was the best they could do. Then Leofric copied it onto good parchment and sent it, carefully sealed, with a servant to the west gate of the Nunnery where it was handed over to the porteress.

Now all they had to do was wait. The future was up to Saint Edburga. And the Abbess, of course.

Based on:

"Nunnaminster: A Saxon and Medieval Community of Nuns" by Graham Scobie and Ken Qualmann. Winchester Museum Service, 1993.

"Hampshire Nunneries" by Diana K. Coldicott. Phillimore, 1989.

"Winchester" by Tom Beaumont James. Batsford/English Heritage, 1997.

"A Picture of Hampshire" by John L. Baker. Robert Hale, 1986.

"A History of Hampshire" by Barbara Carpenter Turner. Phillimore, 1978.

"The Formation of England, 550 – 1042" by H.P.R. Finberg. Paladin, 1977.

"The Beginnings of English Society" by Dorothy Whitelock. Penguin Books, 1977.

Displays and information at Winchester Museum, The Square.

Chapter Six

Basing Castle, 1189

I am deeply concerned about my son, Adam – but then mothers never cease to worry over their offspring, even when they are fully grown. Adam is so head-strong, impetuous and fearless. He takes too many unnecessary risks on the battlefield and, despite his bravery and prowess as a warrior, my heart is filled with dread when I see a messenger clattering into the courtyard on a sweating horse. Always I fear to hear of a death.

My husband, John de Port, departed this life some years ago and I have continued to live here at Basing in great comfort and rich estate ever since. My marriage certainly brought me great material rewards. Indeed, I did not know that such landed wealth as was possessed by the de Ports even existed. As is well known, when Duke William of Normandy conquered this country in 1066 and became king, he brought with him a company of knights. Among these was Hugh de Port, originally from the village of Port-en-Brosse, near Bayeux in Normandy and from which he took his name. Because he was a close and trusted companion of King William, he was granted much land, all taken from the defeated Saxons, which lay in the southern part of England and in reasonable proximity to each other. Those knights less trusted had their lands scattered throughout the shires so that the gathering of soldiers and concerted rebellion against the King would be more difficult. But Hugh de Port was favoured and he held of the King fifty-six manors, all within this shire, as well as other lands elsewhere. He had also been made Sub-Constable of Dover Castle, with Kent lands to provide an income, and continued to hold his own lands in Normandy as well as thirteen properties there as a tenant of Odo, Bishop of Bayeux, who was the King's half-brother. To be a de Port was therefore to be of the élite. And very wealthy.

Basing, where I am now, is the caput (that is, the head) of the de Port lands in England. All the family's estates thus belong to the Honour of Basing and there are few villages hereabouts that do not owe their allegiance to my eldest son, Adam. We do have many relatives in the shire, of course, for the de Ports are good breeders and my father-in-law, Henry, had brothers and cousins living in the vicinity – over at Amport (named after the little river Ann and the de Ports) there is a large brood. Henry's brother, Adam (after whom my own son is named) held de Port lands at Mapledurwell near here, along with Newnham, Up Nately and Andwell. These are all held of the de Ports of Basing, who hold all their lands direct of the King as tenants-in-chief.

Adam is a true great-grandson of the powerful Hugh de Port and revels in the pomp, the riches, the deference, the royal associations. These all delight him but, nevertheless, he is deeply devout. Perhaps this is because he is such a splendid fighter (like most of his family) and is constantly in danger of death or disablement and so needs hearty prayers to keep him whole. When he travels round his Hampshire estates he likes to see that the manor churches are in good order. At Warnford in the Meon valley, for instance, he has paid to have the church rebuilt in good and expensive stone. In other places he has given away whole manors to local abbeys, and has founded priories, some of which are in England and some on his Normandy lands. His own father, John de Port, gave Bramley church and all its tithes to the Abbey of St. Vigor in Cerissy, Normandy, and these are now administered by the Prior and Convent of Monk Sherborne, not far from here.

It is hard to travel in this part of England and not find de Port benefactions. Such giving to the Church was much encouraged by King William, who even gave our own church in Basing village to the Abbey of Mont St. Michel, off the Normandy coast, although we naturally keep our family chapel in the Castle. So I was not worried about Adam's soul – it was his body which concerned me. With all the travelling about and the fighting he was doing, I felt deeply for his first wife, Sibilla, for she had already been widowed once. She was older than Adam and an heiress in her own right, having first been the wife of Miles, Earl of Hereford. When he died she married Adam. It was through her that the Herefordshire lands came to the de Ports, for her inheritance was naturally transferred to her new husband, making us richer still.

When the barons rebelled against King Henry II (this was after the murder of archbishop Thomas Beckett in 1170) his powerful queen, Eleanor of Aquitaine, had encouraged their sons, the Princes Henry, Richard and Geoffrey to rise against their father (Prince John being only about seven years at the time). It was then – to my alarm – that Adam disappeared. I thought he might have been with another rebel, William de Braose, who was a relative of ours through his marriage to Bertha, the second daughter of Miles, the late Earl of Hereford, and Sibilla, later Adam's wife. De Braose had vast estates in Wales, where I have heard he behaved very badly, but I could hear nothing of Adam being with him. It seemed my son had taken all his closest retainers. Those left behind were as much in the dark as was I.

So I worried; Sibilla worried. We both knew there was much treachery and treason among King Henry's court and, with the penalty for both being death, we were doubly concerned.

Then, in the year of Our Lord, 1173, we heard of fighting in France against Louis VII, king of that country. Our estranged Queen Eleanor and her sons, the three Princes, had joined him and were thus virtually at war with their father, the English King, over disputed territories. In addition, the King had trouble with the eldest of his sons, Prince Henry, who his father had crowned three years before as his heir apparent and who was known as the 'Young King'. Inevitably the boy became discontented with not receiving at once the full powers of kingship and, aged eighteen, became resentful of his father's continuing control. The Queen, who we knew quite well from her earlier stay in nearby Wolverton while her husband was in

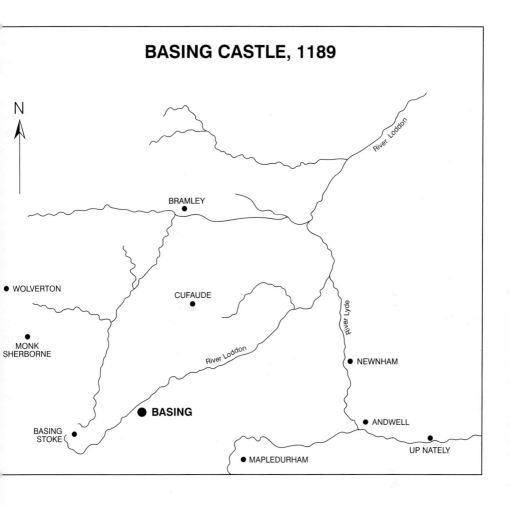

BASING CASTLE, 1189

N

River Loddon

BRAMLEY

WOLVERTON

CUFAUDE

River Lyde

MONK
SHERBORNE

River Loddon

NEWNHAM

BASING

ANDWELL

BASING
STOKE

UP NATELY

MAPLEDURHAM

Normandy (and who ran up the exorbitant expense of £18 for her maintenance while there) was, of course jealous of the King's numerous mistresses. In particular she resented his favourite, Rosamund Clifford (known to us all as the Fair Rosamund) with whom he lived quite openly. Obviously he could not marry her, already having a wife, so he built her various houses, the most splendid being close to Woodstock Palace, outside Oxford. Another was at the Wolverton hunting lodge to which the couple would occasionally come. When Rosamund died in 1176 the king gave much land from his estates at Kingsclere in her memory to the nunnery at Godstow near Oxford, where she is buried.

But still we had no news of Adam. Was he fighting in France? And if in France did he fight for or against his own king? Henry II was a man with a ferocious temper inherited, perhaps, from his mother, Matilda, who had married Geoffrey of Anjou known as the Plantagenet, and who had fought Stephen for the throne of England. So it was not wise to arouse the royal anger. But power is all, and now that the early favour of William I towards the de Ports no longer applied, it was dangerous to oppose the king. Life was thus very insecure for those such as ourselves for, if we judged wrongly and supported the losing side in the power struggle, the penalties were severe. Impoverishment would afflict not only us but our chief followers although the hardship would not extend to the labourers, they being attached feudally to the land and therefore largely indifferent as to who were their overlords.

Those months of waiting for news were very difficult. It is lonely here, despite the outward show of pomp, and with the land so flat, marshy and spring-laden (for the River Loddon is close) the atmosphere is damp, with frequent ague-bearing mists. Most of us suffer rheumatics in our joints – what else would you expect from a dwelling islanded in mud? Our present castle is on a mound with a typical de Port moat and this does aid drainage, but a stone building such as this is colder and more gloomy than even a knight's timber dwelling, small though that might be. And without Adam's robust cheerfulness the rooms echoed emptily.

So I missed him. As, of course, did Sibilla and the wives and mothers of those retainers he had taken with him. Those men were his sub-tenants, owing him obligations as their overlord in the form of military service as fees for their lands.

Many of the knights such as these are little more than country young men mounted on sturdy horses, hoping to win fame, glory and loot on a military expedition. Such adventures are really their only chance of advancement.

I had heard that Adam did have some of his own friends with him, such as William Cufaud and one of the de Scures, and I felt certain that these men – who knew well – would acquaint me of any ill that befell my son. But the waiting was difficult. Difficult, tedious and slow. Then we did hear. He had been in Scotland since 1172 and not in France at all.

At that time King William of the Scots was fighting for total independence from England and to this end had gathered an army – including my son and his men – and marched to take Carlisle. Later they had moved to the east coast but were heavily defeated at Alnwick in Northumberland by loyal allies of the English King, Henry. William of the Scots was captured, but I was told Adam had fled north over the border in the company of Roger de Mowbray. He had remained there for a while, in necessary hiding from the vengeance of his own King and overlord.

I was very troubled by this news, as were we all. How could he return to Hampshire without forfeiting his freedom, for he would have to pass through the estates of many lords who were still loyal to Henry and could thus suffer capture? Luck was with him, however for the king eventually behaved very magnanimously not only to his three rebellious sons (although unforgiving to their mother, his queen, Eleanor) but was lenient with other rebels also, forcing them only to submit to fines. Thus, here at Basing, we were startled one day to find the king's constable at the door who revealed that, although Adam's life was not forfeit, all the lands inherited from his father, John de Port, were sequestered and he was deprived of all income from them. He was also to lose those rich lands which had been the fief of Sibilla in Herefordshire and this would be a great blow to him financially.

So Adam was not to be imprisoned nor beheaded as I had feared. Just to suffer monetary penalties. (Indeed, in 1176 he was fined an additional three hundred marks for trespassing in the king's forests on his way south from Scotland.) But at that time all we needed was to have him actually home. I sent out scouts to locate him so that I might have warning of his imminent arrival but, even so, he took us by surprise, arriving one rainy morning. This was the one clattering into the courtyard which did not fill me with dread! Instead, joy suffused the whole house and I had to exercise great restraint so as not to rush out to greet him before Sibilla could do so. Even on such an occasion, precedence was important. Wives came first.

Our happiness was short-lived, though. Sibilla caught some kind of fever and died. Adam was devastated, for he was not only fond of his wife but must now marry again for he needed an heir. It was thus necessary to seek the king's forgiveness for his disloyalty and to obtain the reinstatement of his lands, for without these he would not be welcomed as a suitor by the fathers of eligible daughters. I was much feared that one of the powerful family of the Earl de Ferrers, who had vast estates in fourteen shires including our own and which owed fealty to their Honour of Tutbury Castle in Staffordshire, would win the greatest available heiress instead of Adam. Something had to be done. I considered all the local families who had marriageable daughters and dismissed them, for none had real wealth or prestige. Even some of their lands were of very poor quality – much of the de Scure estate at Nately, for instance, being of a stiff clay with a clay subsoil, and thus only fit for wheat and beans, and even those, in a wet year, would rot where they were sown. A wet region is this. It is just as well that the de Port manors are well scattered, with enough profitable soils to keep us rich – and hence powerful. From near the southern coast of England to the old Roman roads north of here, we have such a variety of soils and woods, rivers, mills and villages that we are well supplied with foods and men.

It was the summer of the year 1180 that Adam strode into my chamber. "Mother!" he declared. "I am come bearing good news and bad. The King has fined me again, a thousand marks this time, but as I have become betrothed to Mabil, the daughter of Reginald d'Orval, he is being kind. I am to receive back the de Port lands left to me by my father, provided I submit to the fine. I suspect our royal sovereign is short of funds for his French wars!"

I held out my hands to him. I had never heard of the d'Orval family and feared that its members might be impoverished, or at least not as wealthy as we needed.

"I am truly glad!" I smiled. "You need an heir. And am I right in thinking the king has suggested this liaison? The two items of news have come suspiciously conjoined."

He laughed, "He did make suggestions, I admit! I hear that this Mabil is of sufficient beauty. I shall know more when I see her."

"And does she come landed – or impoverished?"

"Oh, landed," he replied airily. "Very landed! It seems her father had married Muriel, daughter of Roger St John, and Mabil is now the heiress of her late mother to the St. John estates – some of which are not far from here at Farley Chamberlaine. On our wedding day I shall hold these very extensive lands by right of her inheritance, and also become lord of the Honour of Lithaire and Orval in the vicomté of Coutances."

"Ah!" I exclaimed. "More lands in Normandy? A rich inheritance indeed! I am delighted, my son. Delighted! Now I hope the child is pleasant and, with you away so often, chaste."

Adam turned restlessly towards the window-opening, through which we could see the summer greenery of the woods beyond the Loddon. "But I am not permitted to keep my Herefordshire lands," he growled. "All Sybilla's lands are still forfeit. More's the pity. There was good hunting to be had and the salmon from the Severn were the best."

"So who has the estates now?" I queried. "The King?"

"No, they've gone to William de Braose. But as the husband of Bertha, my stepdaughter, they are still linked to our family through Sibilla, although I can't see how we can turn that to our advantage. So I have lost – irredeemably, I fear – control over those estates. What a pity Sibilla died! Still, I suppose I am lucky the King has forgiven me, even though only partially. I had expected a blast of the furious royal temper."

"And you gave away the Littleton manor to the Abbey of St Peter in Gloucester, I seem to remember. Isn't that near the St. John lands at Farley Chamberlaine? What a pity! If you had kept Littleton, the Farley manor would have covered an even greater area. But, there! How were you to know your wife would die?"

"Or that I would marry into the St. John family."

Adam turned and strode about the chamber, unable to settle. "Now I must see to my men. And talk to the Steward – hear from him how things have fared. He has, I hope, tended you well? No trouble there?"

When I had reassured him on that point, he knelt briefly, kissed my hand a little abstractedly, and left the room. I sighed. I knew the signs. Adam would not stay in Basing for long but be off – hunting, perhaps, or carousing with his friends. So restless! I would be glad when this new wedding was over and he became a family man again.

I heard that the King was now in Winchester and ordering further work on the Castle. The royal chapel of St. Judoc had been renovated a few years earlier, followed by the kitchens. Then it was the turn of the houses for the king's birds – his precious hunting hawks and falcons. I believe the new work on his own chamber came to £81.8s., with a further £3.10s spent on the repainting. It must be very splendid. And rightly so. It would not do for Henry II, our lawful king, to have properties of less splendour than those of his subjects for, even here, in cold and draughty Basing, the chambers are to be improved. I shall be thankful, for the weather of recent years has been dismal. I am quite convinced that our summers are colder and wetter than they were. On a recent visit I found that Ailward, the king's chamberlain at Winchester, thinks as I do. It seems the rain is washing away the topsoil from the ploughlands, destroying the seedling crops. Weeds are now spreading in, to the ruination of the harvests, and Ailward said he feared a rise in ood prices and the onset of famine. I added that the recent increase in the size of labourers' families will cause problems for we have had few epidemics of killer diseases for a while (God be praised) and, with girls marrying earlier nowadays, the child-bearing years are increased. It is no wonder the number of babies is rising year by year. If a famine does come, I can see there will be unrest among the poor. They will surely starve unless the weather improves and harvests are more productive.

Adam was married in that year of 1180. I did not attend the ceremony and only met Mabil on their return here. She seemed compliant and deferential to her husband and I was well satisfied. The lands she would eventually inherit were extensive and would benefit the de Port exchequer. I waited for the news that she was with child and was delighted when this was brought to me within a few months.

The first child was named William and was a pretty boy, with his mother's fair colouring. I had hoped that he would grow up to be a typical de Port – tough, hardy, energetic and brave – but as the years progressed I could see he took more after Mabil. By the age of seven he was still afraid of horses and showed no aptitude for sport or manly exercises. His playmates, who came here to share his life and be brought up as knightly material under Adam's care, were rougher and more resilient than William. Beside them he appeared almost girlish and I could see Adam's disappointment and his growing scorn.

I discussed the matter with our priest, Father Benedict, and revealed that I considered the boy to be naturally left-handed. "So he must be forced to use his right hand" he told me. "No soldier may use his left – think of the confusion on a battlefield with a close line of soldiers, some with their swords in their right hands and others with theirs in the left. The sword of one would clash with the sword of his neighbour and both shields would become entangled. No, my Lady, William must have his left hand strapped behind him until he uses his right all the time. He is, after all, a de Port and therefore a soldier."

"Poor William!" I murmured. "But you're right, Father. I'll mention it to my son."

So it was that my grandson suffered the indignity of being bound with leather. To my surprise he showed considerable spirit in rebellion. Twice he ran away to hide when he saw the sword-master approach. Once I heard him shout, "I won't be a de Port! I won't! I'll be a St. John! I'll be my mother's son – not my father's!"

He was thrashed, of course. But as he would eventually inherit all Mabil's St. John lands as well as wealth from Adam, we humoured him and allowed him to be called William St. John. Luckily it amused his father, gratified his mother and, surprisingly, seemed to remove a good deal of the boy's fear of failing the de Port image of bravery. Sometimes he used his right hand quite voluntarily, but would give a sideways grin at his parents, especially when he was serving his father at table. Using the correct hand for swordwork was still difficult, though – until he lost a mock fight with his younger brother. It seems they were playing on one of the castle's spiral staircases, with William above as defender. With his wooden sword in his left hand he could not reach round the central newel post to attack his brother below – the stairs, of course, climbing sunwise. After that he realized the importance of being right-handed. Nevertheless, he did not give up his ability with his left, declaring that when mounting an enemy spiral stairway to be left-handed would be a definite advantage, for the newel post would not impede his swordwork. His father laughed, having to agree, and William was back in favour.

Then King Henry II died and his son, Richard came to the throne. I had felt a considerable sympathy for Henry, tyrannical and domineering though he had been, for he had ruled England with a firm hand. He had also done his best to control his French subjects and keep his enemy, King Philip, from taking the English lands in western France. On both sides of the Channel, Henry had had trouble, for the barons here had become increasingly rebellious. Perhaps the worst was knowing that his estranged queen, Eleanor, and his sons, Richard and now John, had all risen against him. With the 'Young King' Henry having died in 1183 and Geoffrey in 1188, Henry II had few supporters in England. Even my son Adam was against him.

But Henry, despite his failings, had brought immense benefits to this country – not least his legal reforms and the creation of the jury system. Now twelve men are chosen to give their opinion on serious criminal cases to the travelling Justices. This is infinitely preferable to the old way of trial by fire, water or battle. (It was the administration of criminal law that had caused the King and Archbishop Becket to quarrel, for Henry had insisted that the clergy were not immune from prosecution.) The king had been a strong ruler without a doubt, even managing to sign treaties with the Irish and Scots which confirmed him as their overlord, so officially ending the fighting against both those countries.

Another law Henry had made was to exchange the feudal military obligations of landowners for a new tax, known as scutage, which paid for mercenary soldiers. How this tax will affect Adam I do not know, for he has not yet paid off all the fine of 1,000 marks and still owes 251 from his debt of 1180. He has little money to spare at the moment. Perhaps this is why he is overseas again, trying to gain favour with this new king.

And King Richard we do not really know – he is hardly ever in this country. Nevertheless, he is immensely popular and held in high esteem by the people. I admit he is of a splendid physique – a golden man – but is clearly more interested in leading crusades to the Holy Land than in governing England.

So with Adam away yet again, I pray continuously for his safe return. Life is nothing without him – eldest sons are very precious and mothers never cease to worry about them, grown-up though they be.

Based on:

The Victoria History of Hampshire', edited by William Page. University of London, 1973.

Dictionary of National Biography', edited by Sidney Lee. Smith & Elder, 1892.

The Crowned Lions: the Early Plantagenet Kings' by Caroline Bingham. David & Charles, 1978.

English Society in the Middle Ages' by Doris Mary Stenton. Penguin Books, 1991.

The Offshore Islanders' by Paul Johnson. Phoenix, 1992.

Companion into Hampshire' by L. Collison-Marley. Metheun, 1948.

A Picture of Hampshire' by John L. Baker. Robert Hale, 1986.

A History of Hampshire' by Barbara Carpenter Turner. Philimore, 1978.

Leaflets from Basing House and various churches.

Chapter Seven

Romsey and Southampton, 1378

I enjoyed myself at the Nunnery. At first, that is. I was not there for religious reasons, having no vocation and no intention of making my vows, even if my father would let me. I was at Romsey Abbey simply to keep me out of the way of the French.

War between France and England had begun again in 1369, but as I was only aged six it had made little impression on me. My father, as a vintner of Southampton and importing Gascon wine for resale in the southern counties, suffered badly from the war, as did all in his trade. Not only was the French army almost at the gates of Bordeaux, which was the main port from which the wine-ships sailed, but a severe plague had hit that region leaving many vineyards untended. In conjunction with local floods and famine, wine thus became extremely expensive and in short supply. Unfortunately many English vineyards had already failed, largely due to the inclement weather. To make matters worse, foreign merchants also stayed away because of the wars and the consequent dangers at sea. This meant that the sweet white wine of Italy was also difficult to obtain. Most vintners were badly affected and we all became considerably poorer. Even King Edward III had difficulty obtaining wines through the merchants. As a result his prisage tax (which he took free in several tuns from all imported wine) was greatly reduced. Consumption of ale at court must have increased considerably.

My father's Southampton house stood in a good position on English Street, having a wide and valuable frontage which was as yet undivided into smaller plots. This spoke of his considerable status. Beneath were great vaults, built largely of stone from the Isle of Wight, there being none locally. Seeking to extricate himself from his present financial difficulties, he had mortgaged the house with another merchant, who was himself owed payment by the king for wine supplied. Unfortunately, the king could not pay either. As a result, several leading burgesses became bankrupt, my father included, for he could not cover the loan on the mortgage. He survived as many did, by indulging in the illegal activity of forestalling (that is, the buying of goods on their way to market in order to resell them at an unfair profit and a higher price to the townsfolk). I think he also cheated over taxes and other dues.

After 1370 the situation began to improve. Foreign merchants returned to Southampton and the wool trade recovered, although the wine trade took longer to do so. Now, however, it was not the English but foreign merchants who dealt in wool – and increasingly in woollen cloth woven in England, rather than in the great sacks from the summer sheep-clip. The seasonal aspect of both the wine and the wool trades caused many complications. When, perhaps by Spring, the supply of these commodities had run out, many dealers were left with money obligations they could not fulfil. Some were reduced to mortgaging future clips of wool or future wine deliveries in order to obtain ready money. And some were bankrupted by so doing. A murrain, which killed the sheep, could wipe out any hope of redeeming a pledge. Likewise, a shipload of wine, fully mortgaged, might be lost through storms or piracy at sea. It was a very difficult time. Even Winchester, that great cloth centre, collapsed into penury, with burgesses leaving the city in despair, as they were leaving Southampton for the same reason. This, of course, left many empty dwellings and burgage plots.

My father, ever on the lookout for financial profit, sought to gain by this. He managed to mortgage himself still further and bought up some of these properties at a very low cost. He then partitioned their frontages, making two dwellings and perhaps two shops, where only one had been before. These tenements he then leased out at satisfactory rents. After a few years we became rich and respected again.

Then, in 1377, Edward III died, still besotted with his mistress, Alice Perrers. As the heir to the throne, the Black Prince, had already died of dropsy, it was the king's grandson who came to the throne as Richard II. In that year, increasingly terrible French attacks began again. And it was then that my father sent me to Romsey Abbey for safety. I was fourteen years old.

Romsey is on the River Test and not far from Southampton and so was the obvious place for me to go – provided the Abbess would have me. Luckily, my late mother's sister was a nun there and this aunt (who I now had to call Sister Anna) persuaded the abbess to take me as a boarder, my father having to pay handsomely for my maintenance. There were only three other boarders. One was Jocata, a girl older than I was; another called Alys who was younger and Robert a small boy aged six. Alys was destined for the cloister, her parents having died in the pestilence of 1360, and her inheritance (which I understood to be considerable in both land and coin) was coveted by her guardian. This guardian could not, however, claim her wealth until she was voluntarily confirmed in her calling and fully professed as a nun. (In Benedictine abbeys, to which order Romsey belonged, the ruling was that no girl could be admitted to the habit and veil until she was aged sixteen, so Alys had another two years in which to make up her mind.)

The four of us shared a dormitory, little Robert being our pet. When he was older he would have to leave the Abbey, of course, but meanwhile we spoilt him, calling him 'Robkins', and giving him as many titbits as we could save unobserved from the refectory table. Not that any of us was kept hungry, for the food at Romsey was plentiful and nourishing, so much of it coming from the abbey estates around the town, as well as from its lands in Wiltshire, Dorset and other places. We usually had meat three times a week and plenty of fish from the Test, on which the Abbess held fishing rights, although she had constant trouble with poachers. Nor in the winter months were we short of fish, as the abbey cart would be sent to Southampton for barrels of red herrings. These last were pickled in salt, the abbey owning a saltern

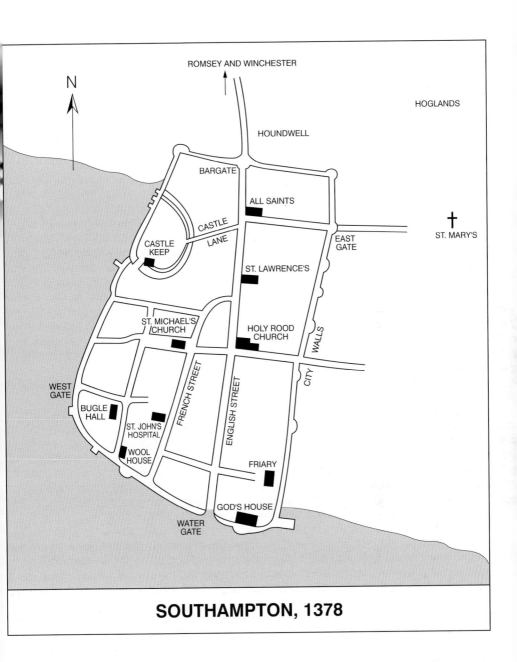

N

ROMSEY AND WINCHESTER

HOGLANDS

HOUNDWELL

BARGATE

ALL SAINTS

CASTLE LANE

CASTLE KEEP

EAST GATE

ST. MARY'S

ST. LAWRENCE'S

ST. MICHAEL'S CHURCH

HOLY ROOD CHURCH

CITY WALLS

WEST GATE

BUGLE HALL

ST. JOHN'S HOSPITAL

FRENCH STREET

ENGLISH STREET

WOOL HOUSE

FRIARY

GOD'S HOUSE

WATER GATE

SOUTHAMPTON, 1378

at Eling, near Totton. As the port of Southampton was much used for the import of foreign delicacies and spices, we were quite accustomed to having our food delicately flavoured with sugar, pepper, ginger, cloves, cummin, nutmeg, cinnamon or other rich delights. In hot summers these are still very necessary as food becomes tainted quickly. The spice ships also brought us rice from the Mediterranean area as well as much fruit including lemons, pomegranates, raisins, walnuts, large amounts of almonds for use in cooking and oranges in season, although these tended to be rather bitter.

Naturally we had to be educated as well as fed, and principally this entailed our learning how to spin and do embroidery. We all spoke French, this being the language of the nobility and upper sort of people, although in my own home we spoke mostly English, my father being only a merchant. As all the nuns came from the upper strata of society, they spoke French from habit. We children could read, of course, for this was essential for religious services and devotional books, and Alys and I could write. We were also taught the Credo, Ave and Paternoster by rote, as well as piety and good breeding. I think we were fairly biddable and obedient as a group – until things happened to Jocate.

She was aged nearly fifteen, and destined to be married to a king's lawyer of Winchester. She had never met him and had been betrothed by proxy, aged eight. Betrothals, being as legally binding as marriage itself, cannot be broken without mutual consent between the parties, so she was now in despair, having fallen passionately in love with the son of the abbey Receiver. She did not see this young man very often, and never alone, but just on those few occasions when he accompanied his father on business. The Receiver was probably the most important of the nunnery officials, running the financial side of the estates for the Abbess and holding various legal courts on her behalf. As a result, his son was well dressed, well spoken and well mannered. His name was Ralph.

Now, in the Abbey at that time were two lady boarders (that is, corrodians) who had paid large sums to the Abbey in exchange for the hospitality of the convent for life. One of these, the Lady Elspeth, was quite old and a widow, but had a certain youthfulness about her and soon realized the situation between Jocate and Ralph. She gave out little hints that she was entirely on their side, although she must have known this was wrong, and contrived to call us to her chamber when Ralph and his father were in the courtyard below, perhaps in conversation with the Reeve. Sometimes such talk lasted for many minutes, with Jocate leaning from the window to attract the young man's attention without his father noticing. That Ralph saw her was certain, for even I could see his face become quite pink.

One day Jocate contrived to drop a kerchief from the window to land at the feet of the Receiver. He picked it up, looked towards the upper room, but saw only the Lady Elspeth, who had speedily replaced the erring Jocate. Without interrupting his conversation, he handed it to Ralph and indicated that he should return it whence it came. By this time Jocate was down the stairs and waiting for the outer door to open. What then transpired I do not know, except that it was several minutes before she returned, her face scarlet and her eyes shining.

Two nights later she was missing from her bed when the bell rang at two in the morning for Matins, the first Divine Office of the day. Even after Lauds, which followed immediately, she had still not appeared. We boarders did not sit in the Choir with the nuns, of course, but among the lay sisters and servants where we recited only the short prayers we had learnt by heart. Naturally Jocate's absence was noticed by these neighbours and a good deal of chatter and speculation broke out among them. After the services were over, the Cellaress, who was responsible for the supervision of these servants (who did the actual work of the Abbey) and in partial charge of the lay sisters, returned to where we were waiting to go to our dorter to finish the night's sleep.

"And where is Jocate?" she asked. "Is she sick?"

As we did not answer, she turned to the servants in dismissal, at the same time upbraiding them for disturbing Divine Office. Then she looked at each of us in turn.

"Not sick, madam," Alys ventured. "But I truly do not know where she is."

"But I do!" little Robkin intervened with a small child's fatal eagerness. "I do! She's run away with Ralph!"

"Is that so?" The Cellaress said slowly, her eyes searching our faces. "Robert, go to bed. You two come with me."

To our considerable distress she led us to the rooms of the Abbess, who had not yet retired to her bedchamber. There we had to explain the situation as best we could. As we left the room afterwards and waited for the Cellaress to join us, I heard the Abbess say, "The Bishop's right, you know. These secular lodgers are but a nuisance. Their visitors and pets and gossiping upset us all. Not to mention their jewellery or silks and winter furs. But there we are! We need the income." Then the Cellaress appeared and the door was closed.

Within the next week word reached the Abbey that it had not been Ralph who had run off with Jocate. It seemed a gang of men had broken into the Abbey precincts at night and caught her as she made her way back from the privy to her bed. It was said she had been ravished and abducted by them, and none knew where she now was. Alys and I were very frightened, for Jocate's fate was not one we relished for ourselves, but when we heard that all her possessions had gone, too, (though how and when, we could not discover) we did begin to question the truth of the rumour. Moreover, it came to our notice that the Lady Elspeth had been dismissed from the house, and we could not help but wonder whether she had aided the abduction in some way. I think she had become bored in the nunnery, her lively mind finding little to occupy it. If she had been a nun she could have made a good career for herself within the Order, elsewhere if not at Romsey, for the Benedictines also held the abbeys of St. Mary in Winchester, known as Nunnaminster, and that at Wherwell in the northern part of the county. The only other Hampshire nunnery was at Wintney, but that was only a priory and of the Cistercian Order. However, I soon ceased to ponder the matter of Jocate for my own life produced a serious crisis.

As I reached the age of sixteen, my aunt became increasingly attentive to my well-being and constantly pressed me to take the veil. "This William Notting you are to marry – a foolish young man. I know the family well. You'll soon tire of him – and of marriage. Fraught with difficulties and unhappiness. Join us here in the Order, where all is peace and tranquillity. You are devout and would add much to the Abbey. Be a nun, my dear niece. Take the veil."

Whenever she spoke in this manner I resisted as best I could without appearing rebellious, but truly I looked forward to leaving and becoming a wife. Helping to look after little Robkin, as I did, had encouraged in me the desire for children. But she would not desist. Increasingly she took me to one side and argued that her sister, my late mother, would be so happy in Heaven to know I had entered the Order. When I shook my head, distressed, she became increasingly vehement and even agitated. On occasion even angry. I could not make this out as there had been no pressure put upon me earlier. The trouble seemed to have begun after I had revealed to her the name of my suitor after a short holiday I had recently spent at home.

I was very distressed by the implied criticism of the family of my intended husband. Like my father, the Nottings had recovered their fortunes and, as burgesses, were living richly in Southampton. William's father was important in the town and a Merchant of the Staple, being in wool. This would be a good marriage for me. Both families belonged to the town's élite, sharing with the others the town's official positions, although neither man had yet been elected mayor. Our upper social group tended to marry their offspring within this circle, just as they tended to have their houses near each other. Indeed, certain streets seemed almost to be reserved for them – perhaps governed by price of purchase or rental. For example, both our houses were in the parish of Holy Rood, fronting onto the eastern side of English Street, not far from the Friary. The other favoured parishes were those of St. Michael and St. John, with French Street and Bull Street each containing fine houses, all splendidly rebuilt after the devastation of the 1338 raid by the French. Turn and turn about, these rich families held the high offices in the town and were the most respected burgesses in the Borough. The Nottings were perfectly well thought of, too, and no scandal had yet mired their name. I could not see why my aunt objected to my marriage to William.

One day, losing patience, I challenged her in a most insubordinate manner to reveal the reason for her disapproval. To my consternation, she covered her face with her hands and stumbled from the room. In a very short time, though, she returned with a nun's veil which she forced upon my head, slapping me hard on the cheek when I went to tear it off. I was then pushed from the room and into the presence of the Abbess. "See!" my aunt said. "She wears the veil! She will be a nun!"

"Reverend mother!" I cried, going on my knees before the Abbess. "This veil has been forced upon me. I have no wish to be a nun. It is my aunt's idea and I am most unwilling to submit to her. Please may I remove it?"

There was a moment's silence and then, to my horror, she said, "No, my child. I think it best that you join us here. But as you are not professed, I think a small hood is more suitable. You will now wear this that I place on your head. People will thus know you are committed to the Abbey and our Order."

At that I burst into tears and was led, weeping bitterly, from the room. Once outside the august presence of the Abbess, I snatched off the hood, threw it on the ground. At that my aunt seized my arm and slapped me horribly about the head and body. From that day on she carried a rod, and should she find me without the hood on my head, would threaten to strike me about the legs and back. I would not have objected to these assaults because such beatings were normal to my life, my stepmother or even my father taking a stick to my back should I be disobedient – submission to authority being the great lesson we all had to learn. So it was not the suggestion of a beating that upset me but my bewilderment at the sudden change in my aunt from a gentle kindness to a strange ferocity. If I had done no wrong, why was I threatened? And why this urgency to make me a nun?

In despair I wrote to my father, telling him of my present situation. The letter was taken secretly to Southampton by the Abbey carter who was to purchase wine. A few days later I was summoned to the main chamber of the Abbess, and found my father, very red in the face, already there. When he saw me in the doorway, wearing the much loathed hood, he gave a roar of anger and, snatching it from my head, threw it into a corner. Then he turned to the two nuns and furiously demanded an explanation.

"She is not veiled!" he shouted. "Nor shall she be! This hood – it was but a farce to make her look a nun already. But she is not, and by God's good Grace, she never will be." He then took a hold on himself and said more quietly, "Tell me the meaning of this. What trick are you playing? I have a right to know." Both the nuns now began to cry but this only made my father more impatient. "Tell me!" he repeated.

The Abbess was the first to recover and she explained that my proposed marriage could not go ahead. At this my father growled in even greater anger. Finally my aunt spoke.

"If I were to tell you in full, I would be breaking the seal of the confessional. When a pestilence struck us some years ago, the Bishop sent a letter declaring that if all the priests had died and there was none to hear confession of the dying, a lay person might suffice. And it was one such confession I heard. The death followed too quickly for me to obtain even a deacon to administer the Sacrament of the Eucharist or that of Extreme Unction but, as the Bishop wrote, in this as in other matters, faith must suffice. Therefore I believe the sins confessed to me were forgiven, although there was no formal Absolution. That is all I may tell you."

My father now stood very still, his anger quite gone. "This – this dying penitent – was a woman?" When no word was answered, he went on, "Was the death due to the plagues that befell us in the year this child was born?" Still no answer came but my father put a hand to his face and hid his eyes. "And the woman? Was she my wife – your sister?"

At this I could no longer stand and sank to my knees, waiting in dread for what was to come.

"Was there fornication? Did my wife lie with another man? Is this child here the result of that great sin – a sin against our Lord God and – have mercy on me – against myself as her husband?"

There was no sound in the room but I did not need confirmation. I knew now what the trouble was. I was not my father's daughter. It could only be that William Notting was my half-brother and no marriage was possible between us. I, too, hid my face in my hands and let the tears run down my cheeks. I was a child of sin. An outcast. Undeserving of any love from my erstwhile father, my family, my friends. I had no life before me, save only to be a nun as my aunt had tried to make me.

At last my father turned to the Abbess. "Forgive me the anger, Reverend Lady. This has tried me sore." And to my aunt: "With great honour you have held your silence. You have told me nothing and the privacy of the confessional is still upheld. This has been a hard position in which you found yourself." Turning to me he said, "Come, child. I have loved you all your life and that love does not cease because of another's sin. Come away home. Pack your belongings and I will send for them. And for now, I shall hire another horse and we shall ride together, forgetting if we can what we have learnt."

So it was that I left Romsey, cowed and deeply ashamed. I was the result of sin, as my father had declared, and thus unfit for normal life among others. The black stain of fornication lay over my soul. Within myself I shrank to a speck of dirt, undeserving of life. I was a child of the Devil, a bastard.

When my father and I reached the outskirts of Southampton, I kept my gaze lowered, fearing to see friends or relatives. Even as we passed through the northern suburbs where the very poorest lived, I looked at nothing. Only when we neared the ruins of the old leper hospital of St. Mary Magdalene did I raise my head, seeing myself as a moral leper. Sin was sin and I was the result of it. An unwanted bastard.

As days went by and I realized my father had not revealed my origins to anyone, not even to my stepmother, I began to regain my balance. Clearly, though, word was now being put about that my marriage to William Notting would not take place. One or two commiserated with me over this, making foolish remarks about there being other young men available for my father to choose. How he had broken the news to William's own father (and mine, come to that) I never discovered. Only the coolness between them indicated anything amiss. On one occasion I did ask my father who he had now chosen for me to marry and was disconcerted to receive but an embarrassed grunt and a change of subject. I did not know why this was so and it was only gradually that I learnt the true position. The town, it seems, had heard of my precipitous departure from Romsey and had confused me with the scandalous Jocate who had disappeared from there. No Merchant of the Gild would wish to have me within his family.

"But I'm not Jocate!" I exclaimed. "Why should I suffer such scorn for an ill I did not do? I ran off with nobody and left the Abbey at my father's behest. Can there be such injustice?"

Clearly there could be. I could see now that I would remain unmarried and twice damned – once for the sinful procreation that had produced me and once for a deed of which I was guiltless. I turned to noisy weeping in my chamber, shunning all social occasions, barely courageous enough to attend services in the church of Holy Rood, where I felt all eyes were upon me.

Then I rebelled. If I was unjustly damned in the eyes of respectable society I would become unrespectable. I would leave home and live among the other outcasts – the paupers, the diseased, the dispossessed – and become truly disgraced but justly despised. In my high defiance I thought of the very poor in the northern suburbs beyond Bargate, and of the hovels beside Hoglands and Houndwell Field where the militia mustered. No person of quality lived there. From living in both those areas however, I shrank, for I knew I could never tolerate the filth, the stench, the people's roughness. So I decided to compromise and, with some shame, thought of the newer buildings around St. Mary's Church, to the east of the town proper. This was once the settlement of Hamwic, founded by the Saxon peoples before they moved south to Hampton, our present town. I could reach that quarter quite easily through the East Gate in the town walls, and by passing all the many shops and lesser commercial properties along St. Mary Street, come to the cleaner suburbs there. I envisaged entering a household of decent people in the position, perhaps, of serving girl or stillroom servant. I was adequate in both those crafts, having been well taught by the nuns for the marriage that was now beyond me. Failing such occupations, I could offer myself as assistant to a craftswoman, who might be running her own business. A full apprenticeship to her would be impossible without the money to buy my indentures or having the backing of some worthy person. But I could be a servant.

I sorted out a few old clothes to wear, the more ragged and torn the better, for I did not wish to be discovered. Finally I was satisfied that I looked the part, although I did take the precaution of adding a belted purse, containing three silver coins of small worth, which I strapped beneath my clothing. I did not intend to starve. The next day, after our morning sop of cake in wine, the house was busy enough for me to leave unnoticed by the side door, which led onto the alley. At once I realized I was too clean. The poor had dirtied faces and hands, their fingernails filled with grime, their hair matted and shoes torn and broken. I took the first turning I could and, sheltering in the shadow of a great warehouse, I mired myself in the roadway. After dirtying my face, hands and clothing in the plentiful mud, I felt more secure. Pulling my headcloth further over my face, I stepped out into English Street. Rather than walk past the houses of friends and neighbours, I took the side turnings and came eventually to East Street. I even began to find all this very exciting – like a game. A running-away to punish the world for treating me so unjustly.

When I tried to pass through the East Gate to reach the safety of the country-side around St. Mary's, I received my first check. There were soldiers at the gate. The year was 1378 and we were at war again. Travellers were now being scrutinised. As unobtrusively as I could, I retraced my steps to All Saints church. I was not concerned with being discovered immediately for this parish was in the northern part of the town, occupied by the poor, and most of the workshops were of smiths. Consequently we had no acquaintances there. I knew I would be unable to escape through the western gates, for these had been blocked up long ago in 1360 for fear of invasion. The Pilgrims' Gate below the castle had also been closed with masonry, as had the postern into John Wytegod's cellar on West Hythe, which had made difficulties for him as he needed the seaward access to bring in his great tuns of wine from the quay. So, with all the smaller gates and posterns blocked, I knew I could only escape through the East Gate (which I had already tried) or the Bargate, which led eventually to Winchester. It was this last that I now decided to try.

As I left St. Lawrence's church, I was jostled by a group of country women coming to the poultry market which was held near there. One woman was laden with a heavy basket and held a long pole on her shoulder from which hung three hens, tied by their feet and squawking loudly. She tried to talk to me but I could not understand a word she said. I must have looked foolish and bewildered, leading her to think I was weak in the head and she began to jeer at me. I did not mind her laughter but I saw it was drawing attention to myself and this I feared. So I ran. And I made the mistake of running down Castle Lane.

The way was filled with workmen, levering great stones into position on the castle gate, which had become very derelict and was now being rebuilt. I came to an abrupt stop, for there was no way out of the lane save into the castle, and there I could not go as it was the great royal storehouse and forbidden to ordinary townsfolk. Moreover, soldiers were lounging about and would certainly question my business. I turned to retreat but a workman caught my arm and held me. I was very frightened but, in my innocence, thought only to be rebuked.

"By the Mass!" cried the man who held me. "Here's a chick worth the plucking! What say you, sweeting, to a fine lad like me?"

I shouted to him to let me go, appealing to the idle soldiery for help. But they only grinned and cheered him on, while his leering face came ever closer to mine. His arm then enclosed my waist and held my struggling body close to his so that I knew his lecherous intent. All I could manage was to pull his hair, ineffectual though that was.

"Leave be, leave be!" a workmate called. "She's as unpractised as any babe who sucks the breast. Not worth your lust."

At that he straightened up. "God's bones!" he grinned. "But you'd be young and fresh in bed!" Then he laughed, pushing me away.

With that I escaped again and, on shaking legs, returned to English Street. I had to pause while a cart passed me, laden with woolsacks and fells. Dodging the carter I hurried to cross the street, only to be stopped by his call.

"Hey, mistress! Is it you? Of Romsey Abbey? I remember you well."

I halted, torn between relief at hearing his friendly voice and despair at my subterfuge being penetrated. How could I have guessed the Abbey carter would be in Southampton?

"How's this?" he went on. "Tattered, torn and dirty? What's afoot?"

I could not answer him at first, not knowing what to say. So I leant against the waggon shaft and lowered my head to the back of the ox, the Abbess not yet using horses for cartage. Then I remembered Jocate and the way in which she was said to have left the Abbey. "I was abducted," I replied tearfully. "Taken from my father's house by ruffians. But I wrenched myself away and fled."

At this point I feigned weakness, and seeing my drooping body he lifted me onto the waggon and bade me settle among the woolsacks. "Here," he said. "Take this clout to wipe your dirty face and hands. We cannot return you to your father's house in such a state."

I began to cry again at the thought of returning home, partly from thankfulness at the thought of renewed security and partly because my life there was still impossible. I was still a child of Satan, badly mistreated by the world. I wanted to enter the house secretly and by the same side door through which I had left, but the carter would not have it. If I had really been abducted I would have been glad of his support, so I had to allow him to bang on our door. Eventually it was opened by my stepmother so I found it convenient to cry again. The carter thus gave all the explanations. When she heard the details of my narrow escape, she cried out in alarm. Turning to the carter she said, "By Corpus Domine, may you be ever blessed," and reached for the purse which hung at her waist. "What a foul mischance! To be abducted, and in full daylight! What has come over the world? So much evil. So much crime."

"Ah, madam." replied the carter, his eyes on the purse from which no coins had yet appeared, "there are too many haunts of vice and ribaldry, all with dicing day and night, and young men drinking more than they can hold. A wicked world it is, with burglary, murder, drunken violence, assaults upon the person (as with your daughter here), the evasion of tax and crooked dealings over weights and measures. And bribery, my lady! That's a terrible thing. From top people downwards as I hear. Even Gildsmen!" This he said with a sly smile and I guessed he referred to my father.

"Yes, yes," my stepmother interrupted, finding a coin of suitable denomination and handing it to the carter. "My thanks to you again, and may the good Lord be with you on your journeyings."

The carter removed his cap and made a small bow. To me he said, "Shall I tell the Lady Elspeth that I have seen you?"

"But – but –", I stammered. "Did she not leave the Abbey? When Jocate went?"

"Indeed, but has returned. Whatever her fault, it has been overlooked. And by coming back, the Abbey does not have to return a portion of her corrody. With money short – "

"Thank you, carter – that will do." My stepmother shut the door on him and turned to me. "And you? What were you doing to be seized in such a manner? To be taken without a shout?"

I dared not reply and so dissolved into tears again until, losing patience, I was dismissed to my chamber and a servant sent to me with washing bowl and towel. Later, of course, I would have to meet my father, and that I dreaded. Especially as I was not sure that my stepmother believed my story. This might be one scandal too many for her.

The next day it became clear what was to happen. I was to be sent to a relative of my late mother's in some far away village on the upper Itchen river beyond Winchester, to act as companion to the old lady. No marriage was mentioned, and worse still, no dowry. Without the promise of a settlement, few fathers would consider any girl suitable for a son to marry. A family's reputation and worth was judged by their generosity on their daughter's betrothal. Money was power and money was respectability. That was why the leaving of money in a will to dower some poor but respectable girl was a favoured act of charity. With no dowry coming to me I would have done better to have stayed at the nunnery and taken the veil. More tears followed and much pleading, but a letter was sent to the old lady and another received after a few days. So I set off, riding behind my father's counting-house clerk, all the weary miles to Itchen Stoke.

After the great seaport of Southampton (and even the little market town of Romsey) this was a poor place indeed – a few houses and a scattering of rotting hovels. And there I stayed for all of six months until, unexpectedly, things changed for me yet again.

The same clerk who had brought me arrived unannounced at the house door with a spare horse and a letter. My supposed father wrote that he wished me to return home to Southampton. A dowry had been found for me after all, and my natural father now proposed I should marry a man of his acquaintance. I was to return immediately so that the formal betrothal could take place. I was both astounded and alarmed.

When I arrived at my old home, the greetings were stilted and very formal. The man chosen to be my husband was to visit the next day and I became very nervous at the prospect. When he was finally ushered into my father's privy chamber, where we were all gathered, I recoiled with shock. He was old. Straggling hair escaped from beneath his fur-trimmed hat, and a wispy beard lay below. I allowed myself to be led forward to receive the ceremonial kiss, hoping that he was too aged to be immoderately eager for the marriage bed and wished fervently yet again, that I had remained at Romsey Abbey and taken the veil. This Thomas de Holebury, grey, old and no doubt slobbery, was repugnant to me. After the betrothal there was a feast, at which I could eat little. Later a servant told me my father wished to see me again. In misery I went to his room. Both my fathers were there. Startled, I made my obeisance to each in turn and waited with downcast eyes for whatever new horror was to come.

"Child," Master Notting, my natural father said. "My sin of long ago has meant the punishment has fallen on you – I am guilty of your present suffering and have had you on my conscience since I was recently told the truth of your birth. Now I wish to make amends and so have arranged this marriage to give you both a respectability and a future. Thomas de Holebury is a good man, a widower and very rich. He does not know your true parentage or my part in that, but has heard that some scandal occurred preventing your marriage to my son William, and this is why a considerable dowry is now necessary. I have passed over to your previous father two tenements I hold in the parish of St. Michael and another in that of St. John, along with some rentals. He will now pass these over to Thomas de Holebury as your dowry and as if they had long been his, and you were his daughter in truth." He paused but I dare not look up. I did not want to marry this de Holebury.

"Child", he said again, "your husband is old but an eminent burgess and wealthy. He trades, as you may know, in woollen cloth and has part share in the ship that carries it overseas. He has many other interests also and he has been parliamentary burgess on several occasions and mayor thrice – which offices, as you know, produce handsome profits. As he has no children, when he dies these will all pass to you. As a very wealthy widow you will be much sought after in marriage – and by younger men. My moral debt to you will then have been repaid, although that to your other father can never be. I will go to my death with that ever on my conscience. I have wronged you both beyond all telling, although I did not know this until your father told me, for your aunt at Romsey Abbey never revealed your mother's secret."

Somehow I thanked him with due reverence and, at a nod from my other father, left the room. When I reached the central hall I stopped. For a moment my emotions were very confused and then unexpectedly, I became excited. I ran up the stairs, along the gallery and so to my own chamber. I remember that I even laughed. When my elderly husband died I knew exactly what I would do with the money. A new charity would be set up, perhaps in his name and out of gratitude, to dower respectable but impoverished girls so they might marry. I would not give to the Friary, nor to God's House, known as the Hospital of St. Julian – other rich people left bequests to those. I would spend my wealth on dowering poor girls.

Meanwhile, if I had to bed with old Thomas de Holebury, it would be no undue hardship. Old men had fancies for young girls. Even our late king, Edward III, had made a fool of himself over Alice Perrers. Now I was grateful to this old man for taking me. And when, after his death, I had spent nearly all my wealth, I could still retire to Romsey Abbey, as had the Lady Elspeth. Or even, I suppose, become a nun.

Another marriage – with a younger man – was not in my mind at all at that point. Later, of course, it was different.

Based on:

"Hampshire Nunneries" by Diana K. Coldicott. Phillimore, 1989.

"Medieval Southampton: The port and trading community, AD 1000 – 1600" by Colin Platt. Routledge & Kegan Paul, 1973.

"Italian Merchants & Shipping in Southampton, 1270 – 1600" by Alwyn A. Ruddock. Southampton Records Series, 1951.

"England in the reign of Edward III" by Scott L. Waugh. Cambridge University Press, 1975.

"The Fourteenth Century, 1307 – 1399" by May McKisack. Oxford University Press, 1991.

"Medieval Women" by Eileen Power (Edited by M. M. Postan.). Cambridge University Press, 1975.

Chapter Eight

Titchfield, 1552

Anne Groves stood up and eased her aching back. "I've done for the day," she told the other women, who were still beside the River Meon, slapping wet linen with wooden paddles against their boards. "I'll be lucky if I can get this lot dry before the rain comes. I'm taking them home rather than spreading them on the drying-green."

She packed the sodden sheets into a wicker basket and heaved that into the handcart she had brought with her. "Anyway," she added, "I have to stop – I've run out of soap."

Pushing the dripping load up the narrow walk behind the church and towards her home in the High Street, she worried about her lack of soap. Making more was not a job she relished. Wood ash was plentiful from the house fire, of course, but mutton fat to mix with it was in short supply. Little mutton was eaten in the Grove household, sheep being kept mainly for their wool. Moreover, much of what pig fat she had saved so far was needed to make the dip for the covering of rushlights – and her store of those was running low, too. Winter was not far off and they would be much needed in the house during dark evenings and early mornings. One rushlight lasted only half an hour or so, and much less if it was burned at both ends as her husband, Nicholas, was apt to do. She never liked to see him place the rush sideways in the holder and light both ends with a taper from the fire. It was true he could see better to do his accounts but she had to make extra lights to accommodate him.

So now as she pushed the little cart home, she worried to which use she should put the small amount of fat she did have – rushlights, or soap for cleanliness? One day, perhaps, she would be able to afford proper bought candles – not beeswax ones, of course, they were far too expensive, but of mutton tallow. Perhaps they would smell less horrible than the rushlights.

As she approached her house she hoped Eliza, her daughter-in-law, would be there. She was strong and could take one end of the heavy sheets and help to wring them out by twisting the linen round and round. It was an impossible job to do on her own. Ah, well! At least the big wash was over for another three months or so. Soon it would be time for putting on thicker undergarments and being stitched into them until April or May. Their present dirty clothing she would do in a week or so, with or without soap.

Over dinner at noon, when Nicholas came in from his workshop and they were joined by Eliza and her two small children, they partook of bread and cheese and slices of boiled bacon from their own pig. As always, Nicholas grumbled that most of the fat had been cut from the meat. He was unimpressed by his wife's explanation that she was saving it to make soap and rushdips.

"If there's one thing I like above all others, it's hot bacon fat," he reminded her. "It's good for me – keeps me healthy. Sees me through the cold of winter and I'd rather be dirty than ill."

It was at that moment that Roger, their son, came into the house.

"Have you heard?" he asked when he had sat down on the bench. "The young King's coming to the Abbey – or Place House as it's called now. Edward the Sixth – old King Harry's boy! Maybe he'll throw golden sovereigns to us villagers!"

"Not a chance!" replied his father. "Money's tight again, I hear. And the boy's advisers, being all Puritans, are mean and grasping. We'll have no more of the old King's pomp and revelry. Right dull the Court is, they say."

Eliza suggested the King was just on a friendly visit to see Henry, the seven year old Second Earl of Southampton, at Place House. "The King's only fifteen, after all, so they're not so different in age."

"Or," her mother-in-law wondered, "perhaps he's just come to pay his respects? Don't forget our first Earl, Thomas, was the King's guardian when old King Henry died. That's when they gave him the earldom for his trouble."

"And," put in Roger, "granted him no end of Church riches – not only the Abbey and lands here in Titchfield, but those of Beaulieu in the New Forest and Quarr Abbey on the Isle of Wight – rich the young Earl must be, and him only seven. A huge income."

"Well, I wouldn't be surprised", Nicholas said thoughtfully, "if they hadn't come to look over our foreshore. It's a right easy landing place for an enemy, such as the French. Good harbouring there is in the Solent, and our stretch of coastline isn't called Titchfield Haven for nothing. Shingle bottom, see, and no cliffs nor rocks. I reckon the King and his advisers is coming to seek out any weak spot in the defences of the realm. He don't want them Catholics here again."

"Either that," added Anne, "or he's in want of a breath of decent air after the stink of London. A weak chest, they say the King has. A bit of salt in the breeze will do him no end of good."

After the news of the imminent royal arrival, the villagers were more than usually interested in Place House. To begin with, in 1538 when Henry the Eighth had set up the Church of England, they had been outraged by the removal of the Catholic Canons from the Abbey and it's conversion to a private dwelling house. Too many of their jobs were dependent on supplying the Premonstratensian Abbot and the Canons with goods and services.

"The Abbey's my best customer," Nicholas Groves had grumbled at the time. "Been making their horse-harness all my life – and my father before me. Now I don't know how I'll manage. No Abbey: no customers. And our house-rent still to pay."

Anne had been more distressed by the change in religion, for the parish church had also belonged to the Abbey. One of the Canons had always been the vicar and they had their own private chapel on the south side of the chancel. Nobody had

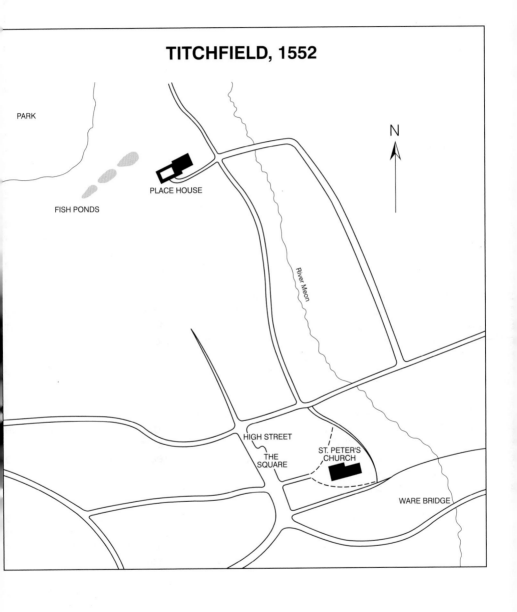

TITCHFIELD, 1552

PARK

FISH PONDS

PLACE HOUSE

N

River Meon

HIGH STREET

THE
SQUARE

ST. PETER'S
CHURCH

WARE BRIDGE

really understood the need for getting rid of the Abbot or his twelve Canons and three Novices – they had all been part of village life and their white robes familiar and comforting. She had also worried that they would starve when they were forced out and was very distressed on their behalf. She later learned that King Henry's Church Commissioners had granted them generous pensions and that her concern had been quite unnecessary. Nicholas always did say she fussed too much.

When the new owner had come, he was much resented. All high and mighty, the villagers thought him. Bowing and scraping to the King to get himself made Lord Chancellor – which meant even more lands and riches. And his family was not all that grand, either. Seemingly their name had been 'Writh', which was now spelled 'Wriothesley' but had to be pronounced 'Risley'. It all seemed very pretentious and foolish. He was disliked even more when he made a very grand gatehouse in the south wall of the Abbey church and drove his entranceway straight across the nave. When he became Thomas, First Earl of Southampton, he was particularly hated. He had too much power and had done away with poor people's livings. A bad man.

But the anger was misplaced. The Earl had employed more men than had the Abbey and no one truly suffered. In fact, Nicholas Groves did well out of the change and even managed to set aside a little money. To pacify his wife he had gone to the Abbey with a few others and his neighbour Sherlond, within a few days of Wriothesley taking over, and offered to buy her a small statue of St. Peter who was patron saint of the parish church. To her annoyance he had failed in this as the price was too high, but he had come away with a cartload of stone.

"More use that be," he told her. "I'll make one of these new-fangled fireplaces and a chimney breast. You'll have much less dust and smoke to deal with. May as well go up in the world a bit, like in other houses hereabouts that are new built. Grander, like. Smoke-holes in the thatch roof seem a bit old-fashioned, now."

And grander was what the village of Titchfield was becoming. The old Abbey had become the splendid Place House, and many eminent visitors with richly dressed followers were now to be seen in the locality. It had also become the Wriothesley's main residence, Beaulieu Abbey having been pulled down following King Henry's orders that its religious buildings were to be destroyed. Much of the stone and lead from those roofs were used to build the defensive castles at Calshot, Hurst and Cowes on the Isle of Wight to protect the south coast from attack by the French. Even Netley Abbey, on the other side of the Hamble river, was ruined for the same reason. Its new owner, Sir William Paulet, the first Marquis of Winchester and owner of the great Basing House, built a dwelling for himself within the monks' church. Sacrilegious, the villagers thought it.

And now the King himself had come to Titchfield to visit young Henry, the Second Earl. Anne knew that it was not the first time that a monarch had been here – the land, after all, had been royal land for many years. She had been told that their five day fair had been granted by King Henry the Sixth when he had married Margaret of Anjou in the Abbey church. And before that, Henry the Fifth had stopped here on his way to Agincourt. Titchfield was used to nobility. The little Meon provided a convenient tidal port for journeys by sea, although the villagers were aware that the river was beginning to silt up and might become unnavigable in the future.

With so many strangers at Place House, the Groves family had prospered. There were many profitable requests for Nicholas to make fine new trappings and saddles for their horses and, as Roger was now out of his apprenticeship to his father, he also began to accrue money. Nevertheless, Anne was puzzled to see Eliza wearing little touches of velvet on her gown and Roger sporting a more fashionable ring in his ear. These things spoke of wealth rather than a working man's wage, increased though that might be. So wealthy did it seem Roger had become, that his mother fretted. Once she had spoken to Nicholas about it.

"Husband, how is it that son Roger is so well supplied with coin? Is trade so profitable? And if it is, where are the gew-gaws and trinkets that you could give me?"

Nicholas stared at her for a long minute, then said, "Leave him be, wife. Mayhap he won money at dice. Now that the Church is not on our backs so much – the White Canons having long gone – we're less burdened with what is sinful. Dicing seems but a little sin, and if Roger's afflicted that way, then it's not our business to condemn him."

"But I worry," Anne declared. "I've no wish for a gambler in the family, and if Roger is one, then I've not brought him up rightly. Gambling is not good."

Her husband did no more than grunt and urge her to drop the subject. "He's a grown man. Treat him like one."

But Anne kept watch and noticed every addition to their clothing. She even checked on the length of time Roger spent away from home. How long would he need to win at the cards? An hour? Two? She was also troubled by the thought he might be wagering more than he could afford to lose on the throw of a dice or the fall of a card. The fear of debt lingered long in her mind. Eliza had two babes now – little Alice and infant Jack – and if too much money was owed against too little security, how could they be bred up in comfort?

Then a thought struck her. If he was not gambling, perhaps he was stealing? There was enough temptation in the village now with more folk having fatter purses. Horrified, she again reviewed her moral training when he was a lad. Had she failed there, too? Not taught him the commandment: "Thou shalt not steal"?

Anxiously she began to take note of the nights when Roger was late home. It was easier to steal at night when the darkness would hide him from the Constable's lanthorn. At first, the nights he was gone appeared to be haphazard. Then she realized they coincided with high tides in the Solent. Had she not been the daughter of a cockle-gatherer on the shore, such a thought would not have occurred to her. Now she remembered how, as a child, she had gone with her father to the strand when the tide was low, even if their only light was the moon. There they had raked up the shells to sell from pails of saltwater in the market the next day. Cockles were ever favourites, even with the Canons of the Abbey. So could the tides have a link with Roger's late nights? Not the low tides, perhaps, but the high?

Then she knew! Horrified, she realized he was tied up with smuggling and was using the tidal flow of the river to bring in a boat of greater depth than normal. Surely illegal and untaxed goods could be unloaded at the inn and sold on from there? Would there not be a tidy profit for those involved either directly or as part-owners of the vessel? No wonder Eliza was bedecked with velvet! Or that Roger was sporting a new jewel in his ear!

But smuggling was a crime, carrying horrendous punishments. Anne's hands shook as she kneaded the bread dough. Heaven preserve them all! Why did a son of hers have to slip into bad ways? Where had she failed in bringing him up to be a decent, God-fearing boy? As a lad he had been docile and biddable, ever cheerful. Fond of company, it was true, and later of dancing and lusty singing with the other young men. But not a smuggler! Not a criminal! Surely? And supposing he was suspected and ran away – the Constable would set the hue-and-cry after him and all the villagers would be bound to give chase. Oh, the shame of it!

She was certain the smuggling itself would be of untaxed cloth going out and French wine coming in. Foreign ships were always in the Solent and who was to tell where they were at night? With Southampton being such a successful port, with it's great stone Custom House near the quay, the King's Collectors of Duties being so vigilant, and his comptrollers keeping such strict accounts of duty to be paid to the Exchequer, the temptation to evade tax and make extra profit was great. But that her Roger should run the risk! It did not bear thinking of. It was not even as if he could escape capture by seeking permanent sanctuary in Beaulieu Abbey, for that legal right was done away with when the monks were turned out and Sir Thomas Wriothesley bought the estate from the King.

A few nights later, high tide fell in the early hours of the morning. She slept very lightly, waiting to hear the drop of the door latch should Roger let himself out of the house. Then, fighting sleep, she did hear him leave. Covering her nightrobe with a warm cloak, she hurried down the stairs. Finding her pattens, she slipped them on over her shoes once she was outside the house. Cautiously she felt her way along the street towards the river. The inn at the Warebridge was in darkness but dimly she could see movement at the high-tide wharf nearby, although unable to distinguish Roger. With so many people about she became scared and retraced her steps, worrying all the while that the Night Watchman would see her or that she would set the dogs barking.

A few days later a servant from Place House was seen to be knocking on doors down the street. Apprehensively, Anne stood in her own doorway, shaking out a mat to give her an ostensible reason for being there. Seeing her, the man came across.

"Mistress," he said. "I'm asking for lodgings for two gentlemen who have come with Sir John Cheke, the King's tutor, and Place House hasn't rooms enough. Can you help me out?"

Anne thought quickly. Dare she ask strangers to the house if Roger was truly a smuggler? To do so would be a quite unnecessary risk. As she hesitated, Nicholas came through from his workshop and was told of the man's request.

"Of course we can help," he said. "I imagine there'll be good payment for such short notice? And with us not being a regular lodging house?" Reassured on this point, he turned to his wife. "Put them in Roger's chamber. He, Eliza and the little ones can bed down in the hay shed. They'll be all right there, seeing as how the weather's still mild."

Thus the matter was taken out of Anne's hands. She was relieved that Roger would now be restricted in his night-time expeditions and so, with moderate content, she found her worries eased.

That evening the two men, Jonathon Plester and Peter Morrisey arrived. They were young men of about Roger's age and fitted easily into the household. Jonathon was horse groom to Sir John Cheke and Peter a body servant.

"How's the King, then?" enquired Nicholas as they sat over the evening meal. "He's delicate, I've heard."

"Used not to be," replied Peter. "Until two years ago he was healthy enough."

"And athletic," his fellow added. "Loved being out on horseback. Developing into a fine swordsman, too. A shame he's been took ill."

"And your master? Sir John Cheke? Easy to work for, is he?"

"Oh, aye! And devoted to the King – as the King is to him. More like father and son than was the case with his real father, old King Henry. Having his education from Sir John has been a pleasure for the boy, I think. Leastwhiles, there's never any trouble getting him to study. Easier than with those other tutors – that Dr Cox and then Roger Ascham, clever though they be."

"With the boy's mother dead – poor little Jane Seymour that was – the lad needs someone to be fond of," Anne murmured sentimentally. "It must be hard, being royal."

"Well, he's king now and can favour who he wants," her husband remarked briskly. "But what we want to know is why he's down here at all. Not Court business, clearly. Is it the hunting? The First Earl made the great park at Place House even greater after he took over the old Abbey. Took over a lot of our ploughland too, where we had our strips. And that wasn't right – caused a deal of trouble in the village. We was all farming in the way called 'champion', having our strips dotted about in the common fields. Instead of them, we were given blocks of land near Hunt Pond already enclosed with fences, for farming 'in several' as it's to be known. A poor deal, that was. Poor soil, you see. Untilled. No dung ever spread there – just waste-land, really." Nicholas sighed heavily. " I know I'm a saddler and harness-maker but I still need my strips. How else can I keep us in corn for the bread? Or have somewhere to graze the cow?"

Peter Morrisey leant forward. "But I've heard enclosing land makes for better farming?"

"Aye," Nicholas replied, "but there's little enough proper farming going on in the Earl's new park! It's all pasturing of sheep. On land that once gave food and employment to most of the village. Ploughs aren't needed now, no sowers in the Spring, nor harvesters at the end of Summer. No end of men out of work because of it – had to go on the Poor Rate. Charity, that is. Or they've moved to the towns, of course. To Portsmouth, Southampton and the like. England's changing, it seems to me. And all for sheep and their wool, with woollen cloth fetching such high prices now. Farming is not the same as it was. Not the same at all."

"Get-rich-quick landlords they are," Roger added. "A new breed of men. Land's all for private profit now – not for granting us our livings." Then he laughed, "No wonder we all go poaching at night in the Abbey's old fishponds! Especially for the big fat carp the First Earl put there!"

His mother glanced at him sharply. Was this what he was up to at night? Not smuggling, after all? Poaching was not much of a crime, and fishing least of all. The village treated it as routine, even though care had to be taken not to be caught. A wave of relief washed through her and she relaxed. Maybe she had brought up Roger well enough, after all. She smiled at him across the table. He was a good son.

Later her pleasure became somewhat muted when she wondered where the poached fish had gone. Sold, perhaps, for coin? And hence the finery Eliza now wore? Anxiety crept up on her again as she puzzled over the matter. However, she began to listen to what the others were saying and gathered that the two visitors were ardent Protestants, for they were talking much of the change in religious observances.

"No more Popish practices!" Jonathon Plester commented with relish. "Just look at Place House – the Earl's great entrance gate built right across the monks' old nave! You couldn't ask for a statement of more contempt, could you? And Netley the same, with the Marquis of Winchester's new house right inside the Abbey building! 'Down with the Catholics', that's what both these houses say. Good Protestant houses! Why else would the young King come to Titchfield, him being so strong in the new beliefs?"

None of the Groves family replied. There had been no quarrel with the old faith. Indeed, Anne missed it.

Roger now excused himself and went out to the yard. His father threw another log on the fire, while Anne busied herself with refilling the men's tankards.

"Why the silence, friends?" asked Jonathon.

Nicholas cleared his throat. "Well, the Abbey was good to us villagers, you see. In a way we miss the Canons. Not their faith," he added hurriedly. "We're all good Protestants here – and we like the services being in English now. But we'd grown up with the Abbey, and they were charitable to us in sickness or hardship. They even taught a few of the local boys to read, and when the plague was hereabouts they did their best for us. Couldn't help folks from dying, of course, but they did attend those afflicted. Prayed over them till their deaths. So, you see, we miss them a bit – although we attend the new services as we're meant to."

"That's as well," Peter said drily. "With the King here it would not be wise to go back to the old ways. His advisers are very earnest in seeing the country changes its habits – and it would do you no good to be reported for Catholic tendencies." Then he changed his tone and said more cheerfully, "But enough of such things! We're at ease here and wish you all well."

But Anne drew in a breath. Be reported? For what? These men must be spies! Come to check on the beliefs of the common people and other crimes. She thanked God that Roger was only a fish poacher and not a smuggler or a thief. Life was so very uncertain, what with new laws and new religious ways, and it would be so easy to commit a crime without knowing and be put in the lock-up for it.

Now she wished the two lodgers away. She could do without their money, even if she had to feed them for nothing. She was fussed, and that was the truth of it. Restlessly she wandered the room, finally leaving as Roger had done, murmuring about seeing to her grandchildren out in the hayshed. Pulling a cloak over her shoulders she went across to where Eliza was settling the little ones. Finding Roger there she went close to him and, in a low voice, begged him not to go poaching any more.

He looked at her in surprise. "But I don't! Not now. What do you mean?"

"That Peter and Jonathon – they're spies! On the look-out for law breakers! Government men, I think. So don't go poaching or anything like that. I beg you – for the children's sake – stay on the right side of the law!"

He asked her why she was so worried.

"Because of the bits and pieces you've bought Eliza. I've a terrible fear they weren't come by honestly."

Roger laughed and turned away. "Oh, those!" he replied. "I'll tell you now if you'll keep it to yourself."

When she nodded, he went on, "P'raps you don't know this, but the young Earl's been brought up a Catholic? A lot of the family still are. With the King and his men coming, it was thought better to take certain items out of Place House. Crucifixes, chalices, images and such. Didn't want them seen by the Protestants.

So I was asked to put them on a boat at Meon wharf on certain nights and on another night to see the priest got safely away. That's all, mother. That's all I did! And was paid for it!"

Anne collapsed into a pile of hay. "Well!" she exclaimed. "Well!" After a moment she added, "And there was me thinking you was stealing or gambling or smuggling or poaching! Thinking I'd brought you up all wrong – and should have smacked you harder when you was little!"

Then she laughed. "All that worry for nothing! What a fool I am! What a fool!"

Based on:

"Titchfield: A History", edited by George Watts. Titchfield Historical Society, 1982.

"Titchfield: A Place in History", edited by R. Wade and G. Watts. Titchfield Historical Society, 1989.

"Companion into Hampshire", by L. Collinson-Morley. Methuen and Co. Ltd., 1948.

"Dictionary of National Biography", edited by Sidney Lee. Smith, Elder and Co., 1900.

"England Under The Tudors", by G. R. Elton. Routledge, 1992.

"Elizabethan Life in Town and Country", by M. St. Clare Byrne. Alan Sutton, 1987.

"Beaulieu: Palace House and Abbey", by Lord Montagu of Beaulieu. Montagu Ventures Ltd,. 1986.

"The Victoria County History of Hampshire", edited by William Page. University of London, 1973.

Leaflet from St Peter's Church, Titchfield.

Chapter Nine

Alton, 1653

The battle had been on the thirteenth of December, in the Year of our Lord, 1643. That was when I was wounded and part of my left leg shot away by a Royalist musket ball. When I recovered consciousness I found myself here, in the house of Esther Morgin and her parents, in a side street of the little market town of Alton.

Originally, I was from London and a year before had joined the Parliamentary army, enrolling in the Yellow Auxiliaries of the London Brigade. In those days I was but twenty years of age and full of the high ideals of youth. It seemed to me that this Civil War, begun a year earlier, was to bring true democracy to England. More power must be given to Parliament and less to the King. The voices of the ordinary people should be not only heard but taken notice of. We had as much right to influence government policies as anyone else. I don't think there were many people who wanted King Charles deposed and certainly not killed. We just wanted an agreement with him that would give us a say in how we lived.

As no regiment liked to fight outside its own area, various associations had recently been formed, with Hampshire (in which county Alton lies), Surrey and Kent forming the South-Eastern Association, and our London Brigade fought alongside them. The weather had been bitter cold for some weeks but despite this, we had been marched to besiege the great Royalist centre of Basing House, the stronghold of Sir William Paulet, Marquis of Winchester (known as 'Old Loyaltie' because of his devotion to the Stuart cause). When we arrived within sight of the huge house, we had to sleep in the fields, despite the driving rain and frequent sleet. The country folk were possibly enured to such conditions, but we Londoners were used to a roof over our heads and dry beds. What made things worse was that the siege dragged on for weeks, for we could not capture the place – it was too well defended with very intricate star-shaped earthworks. We understood that the garrison was composed of two regiments of Foot and a troop or two of Cavalry.

Our commander, General William Waller (who, as it happened, was a cousin of the Marquis and a close friend of the Royalist General Hopton) ordered a strong bombardment but, as it did little good, he sent forward five hundred Musketeers to seize farm buildings next to the north garden of the house. These were eventually captured and set alight. The Royalists, however, counter-attacked, driving our men away from the burning buildings. I was glad not to be involved, our London Brigade watching from nearby Cowdrey Down where we stood and shivered. A soldier in sodden clothing cares little for battles, so we sent a deputation of officers to General Waller to ask to be returned to London. This was not granted but we did retire to nearby Basingstoke, which provided shelter but, as we had received no pay for weeks, we could not much enjoy.

Then Waller announced there was to be yet another attack on Basing House. We grumbled, of course, but when he told us he would lead one of the attacks himself, we felt obliged to be more willing.

Our advance took us right up to the house walls, which we thought would give us protection. Not so! The women inside had climbed onto the roofs and threw down stones and bricks. Many of these landed on our heads, causing many serious wounds. When it became too dark to fire our muskets with any accuracy, the order was given to retire, and this we did with much gratitude although it meant another night in the open. A few days later one of Waller's officers made a grievous mistake, leading his men into an ambush. He was killed along with many others. Another calamity occurred when we were advancing across the open park land to the south-west of the house. The orders for firing were wrongly given so that our rear ranks fired on those in front, thus killing their own men. Horrible, that was. We lost seventy or eighty good soldiers in this way, a loss we could not well sustain. We were very discouraged. Sad and discouraged. It seemed too much of a sacrifice just to assert our political rights over the King.

After that, we left for Farnham Castle. It seemed the Royal army under General Lord Hopton was advancing towards Basingstoke and, with many of us now wishing only to go home, Waller did not feel it wise to stay and fight. I think he feared a mutiny.

At Farnham we had dry lodgings but little rest. Word came that Hopton was now advancing on us with massed regiments. Not all our men had yet arrived – some, we feared, were refusing the call to arms – and clearly we were about to be defeated. I seriously considered changing sides, as many were already doing, officers among them, for no one wanted to die at the end of a sixteen foot pike or be blown to pieces by musket fire.

We were rescued, though. Many said by the Lord Himself who had heard our prayers, for a thick mist covered us all morning, preventing the enemy from attacking. With visibility so poor nobody dared fire. We all wore regimental marks, of course, so that we could tell friend from foe, but in a fog there was insufficient time to check them out. The officers were easier to see as they wore wide sashes across their breast armour or round their waists, but we foot soldiers wore only ribbons on our hats that were the colours of our regiments – in our case, yellow. Our standard had much of yellow also, and in summer we would tuck yellow flowers in our hatbands, while the Green regiment used sprigs of leaves, and the White regiment pieces of white paper or white cloth. We had field-words, too. Passwords, they were, but it was easy to listen to the enemy and use theirs ourselves to trick them. Sometimes our colours were changed to fool the other side. Occasionally the stratagem worked.

While we were at Farnham, winter came on apace. Not snowy, but damp and raw. General Hopton moved his Royalist army to three towns in Hampshire and

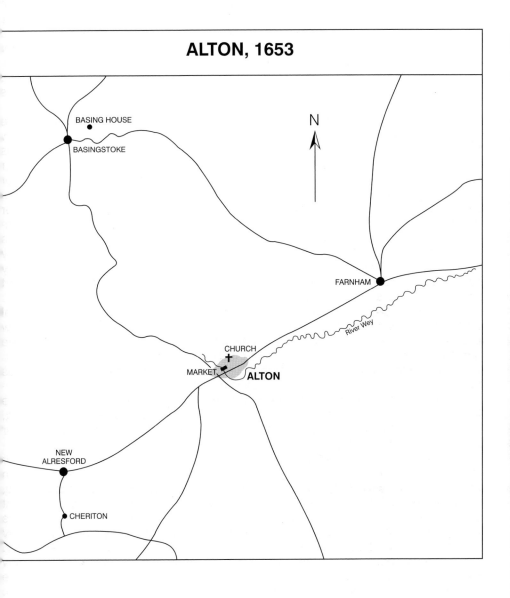

ALTON, 1653

N

BASING HOUSE

BASINGSTOKE

FARNHAM

River Wey

CHURCH

MARKET ALTON

NEW
ALRESFORD

CHERITON

another section to Arundel in Sussex for the winter. To our delight, we received reinforcements – Sir Arthur Heselrige's regiment of Foot with its blue colours, and another from Kent, who were Sir William Springate's White coats. Now we felt sure General Waller would let us go home as we had done our time and he had sufficient troops to replace us. But it was not to be. In preparation for our departure, we had mustered in Farnham Park and waited there all day, bored and cold. We were neither discharged nor paid – and the lack of pay was of a growing concern. There was no way we would allow ourselves to be disbanded until we had received all arrears due to us. We had to live, after all. As dusk fell, Waller arrived and told us we would not only be discharged but receive our pay – as he had promised – but he did stress it would be a discharge without much honour as our efforts against the enemy had seldom prevailed. He asked us then to fight once more, and in a battle which would surely bring us credit. We debated this proposal and most of us agreed to do as he asked. The battle was to be at Alton.

Waller then performed a clever manoeuvre by marching us all night as if we were returning to Basing. After a couple of miles we changed direction and, in a secluded and wooded valley, we turned, going completely beyond the town. By the morning of Wednesday, the thirteenth of December, we approached Alton from the west, the enemy expecting any attack to be from the opposite, Farnham, side.

There could be no set battle, of course, for we had to fight street by street all through the town, suffering greatly from Royalist muskets posted in upper rooms of various houses. Our worst obstacle was a great brick house, not far from the church, from which very rapid fire rained down on us and caused considerable damage to our men. We had previously fired the thatch of several houses and, under cover of the smoke, managed to defeat a sizeable number of Royalists in the market square, the wind being with us. A Royalist resident of the town even set fire to his own house in the hope that the smoke would confuse us. Indeed, it did so sufficiently to allow the Royalist commander, Colonel Boles, and his men to retreat up the hill towards the church where they had previously built protective earthworks. From that position they fought bravely, but finally were driven into the churchyard, still fighting valiantly and shouting their cry of "Charles!" In reply we yelled "Truth and Victory!" but without the arrival of our Red and Green Regiments, who had crossed the little River Wey and come to our rescue, victory might not have been ours.

Finally, Boles and about eighty of his remaining men retreated into the church itself. They had left some muskets propped against the churchyard wall with their muzzles showing over the top and we, fearing an ambush, did not advance. Only when Sergeant Guy of the Red Regiment ventured through the gate did others finally follow. All this time we were being fired on from the church windows, the enemy soldiers having built platforms inside to stand on. They had closed and barricaded the church door so we threw hand-grenades through the shattered windows, and finally gained entry to the church. There we attacked with halberds, swords and the wooden stocks of our muskets, slaying many. Clearly outnumbered, some surrendered. One exception was their leader, Colonel Boles, who had been forced to retreat up the steps of the pulpit. From there he slew near on ten of our men with his sword before he, in his turn, was cut down and killed. With his death, the remaining Royalists lost heart and laid down their arms, becoming prisoners.

It was only then that I realized I was badly wounded myself and losing much blood. I had a musket wound which had taken away part of the muscle of my left leg and I think I fainted clean away. It seems that our troops then began to clear the church of dead and wounded (which is when I was taken in by the Morgins) and replaced us with all the prisoners. I gather that later these were coupled together and marched to Farnham. There were between eight hundred and nine hundred in all, although more were added by our horse regiments. They had been following the Royalist Lord Crawford, who had managed to escape with his Cavalry and had headed for Winchester. I was told that in all that fighting we had lost not more than two dozen, although of course, there were many wounded. The enemy dead numbered between fifty and sixty, I believe. It was a great battle and a great victory for Parliament, particularly as it closed the road towards London to the King. After resting at Farnham, our troops were paid off and disbanded, having refused Waller's request to continue to Arundel.

In the Morgin household I was well tended. The family were not Royalist, although most of Alton was, which is why they had offered to nurse me back to health. This they did with great care, although my leg will never recover completely and I shall always be lame.

Mistress Morgan offered to send a letter to my parents in London, so I wrote a note and she found some military man to take it to them. Her daughter, Esther, was about seventeen at the time and, inevitably, we spent a good deal of time together. Naturally, I worried about my future life and, especially, about gaining a livelihood. When I had been in London I had been apprenticed to a printer, as my education had been reasonably good, but I had not yet completed my obligations to him when the War began. Perhaps when my wound was healed I would be able to find employment here in Alton in the same trade. I would need to convince a printing-press owner that I had completed my apprenticeship and was well qualified. It was a good trade, for printing had become very profitable since war had been declared.

Everywhere one went there were now pamphlets, leaflets, broadsheets and periodicals in abundance. In earlier years government censorship had prevented the free publication of all but foreign news, so now there was a veritable flood. We were deluged with printed sermons and speeches, proclamations and ordinances, libels and refutations – the war seemed to be carried on in words as much as with bullets.

I was not worried about finding lodgings when I was better because the Morgins made it clear that I was welcome to stay. They knew I would recompense them once I was earning again. Moreover, we had many attitudes in common, they being (like myself) Independents in religion. We did not follow the Church of England nor the strictures of the late Archbishop Laud, but rather preferred the complete independence of each congregation. This is where we differed from the Presbyterians for, although both sects followed the teaching of John Calvin, we did not agree with his system of ecclesiastical government. Unfortunately, because of our belief in the necessary freedom of religion, many other sects sprang up.

While my leg slowly healed I made myself useful helping Master Morgin with his accounts. He was a builder in a small way but was now beginning to expand – the town was full of buildings damaged in the recent fighting and he saw plenty of work opportunities ahead. Esther was her mother's helper as a seamstress, for they made clothing to sell at the town's weekly market. The items they disliked making the most were the working men's smock frocks, for the material was coarse and hard to stitch.

Inevitably I fell in love with Esther, and to my great pleasure, she with me. We planned to marry when I became better placed financially – not a church wedding of course, because those were now banned, but before a meeting of our congregation. Meanwhile, we had the pleasure of being close to each other, although her parents were strict about showing our mutual affection. We were, after all, of the Puritan persuasion and they kept a very strict eye on us both – which was difficult to suffer for we were both young, and Esther especially was full of life and a merry girl. So merry, in fact, that there were times when I worried she would get across the authorities and fall into trouble. Not that her behaviour was wild – she was just very forthright in her views and refused to be subdued. Politics and religion were the two topics on which she liked to express opinions the most, and those were the most dangerous.

"Why," she would complain to me, "should you – as a man – be allowed to voice your ideas when I'm not allowed to? Does my being a woman prevent me from thinking? And having thought, prevent me from voicing those thoughts? Surely we're all equal under God? If He gave women minds – as He did – surely He expects us to use them?"

"Of course we're of equal value," I would reply. "But God created men the stronger so as to have dominion over women – to be the head of a family."

"And what's that to do with voicing my opinions? I haven't said that when I'm your wife I'll go against your wishes or disobey your commands. You can be head of the family, if that's what you wish. All I ask is to be allowed to voice my own thoughts. Surely you don't want a mealy-mouthed, empty-headed woman as a wife?"

"No! No!" I would cry. "It's just the decency of the situation. Of proper behaviour. Of family honour."

"And my honour? Does that count for nothing? Does the honour of a woman lie only in not being free with her sexual favours? My honour lies in much more. I am a child of God – not a man's inferior. I have chosen you to love partly because of your ideas. Do you not love me for mine?"

That was a hard question to answer and I did not attempt to do so. Instead I laughed and turned the subject. I knew that Esther, when in a contentious mood, was beyond control. Besides, I was unaccustomed to this new liberty expressed by women and found it hard to countenance. It was all due to the war, I was sure. Now that there was freedom of thought with regard to the monarchy, the King as head of the country was seen as less awesome. In the same way, allegiance to the Church was overthrown and the cry was for separation of Church from State. With no recognized authority over us, I supposed it was natural for women to break out. But I did not like it. Not at all. Perhaps I had been at fault in bringing home copies of pamphlets and other literature from the printer's shop where I was now able to work for a few hours a day. Maybe I had been infecting her mind with unsuitable writings, for some of them seemed very outlandish, even to me, and all were politically biased one way or the other – that is, if they did not appear to be written by lunatics.

It was about this time that I had news of the continuing war. Just as our battle in Alton had blocked one Royalist route to London, so in the following year of 1644 the great battle of Cheriton blocked their retreat to Winchester. I was greatly cheered by this information. Later there was news of a better-trained Parliamentary army coming into existence under their leader, Lieutenant-General Oliver Cromwell. That was in 1645. It was to be called The New Model Army and the soldiers were to wear proper uniforms and receive regular pay. In exchange they had to submit to a strict discipline and conform to exacting regulations.

I heard that earlier there had been an attempt to sort out the trouble with Scotland. A 'Solemn League and Covenant' had been drawn up but the King had refused to sign it as he knew he would be required to favour the Presbyterianism of the Scots, and this he was loathe to do. So the Scottish army invaded England. All this came to me in a very piecemeal fashion. There seemed to be battles going on all over England, with defeats and successes for both armies. Some uprisings were in favour of the King but elsewhere his generals surrendered to Parliament. The news was very confusing but gradually it became clear that we were winning and that Charles would have to bow to the wishes of Parliament. When he was captured by the Scots, after escaping from Royalist Oxford in disguise, they sold him back to Parliament and he became their prisoner.

I was delighted to hear that almost the first thing the members of Parliament did was to vote for the abolition of the Book of Common Prayer. Then they abolished the offices of bishops and archbishops. Now the country was free from the hated Church of England and we were able to worship how we wished. As I understood it, few of the Parliamentary leaders wished to depose the King – they wanted to enter into negotiations with him so that he remained on the throne but did not rule by himself. Apparently, on his journey south as a prisoner, people rejoiced to see him again and he was greeted enthusiastically, even by Puritan gentry. He was still their King, and there were uprisings in his favour in various parts of the country and even in Scotland.

In the confusion of the political situation, it was becoming clear that there was serious unrest in the country. Judging by the pamphlets I was now printing, many people of all social sections were becoming tired of the uncertainty. They were rejecting the Presbyterians and their Calvinist teaching that human lives were pre-destined for either eternal salvation or eternal damnation, and even to me, this seemed to be an outrageous idea. If, whatever we did, we were already allocated to one fate or the other, why repent or attempt to improve behaviour? The doctrine of pre-destination did not attract me at all.

Then we were into what was really the Second Civil War. Not that this affected us in Alton – the troubles were far away in South Wales, Kent, Essex and against the Scots in the North West. I don't believe this war lasted more than a few months in the summer of 1648, but it did illustrate how disturbed and confused the country still was. We couldn't settle down and be peaceable amongst ourselves.

And this was true of the relationship between Esther and myself. We argued too much. I felt she was stubborn in her opinions, and she felt I had a closed mind and an innate prejudice against the worth of women. To some extent she was right. I had been brought up in the belief that women, and especially wives, were sub-ordinate to men and should be meek and obedient. Esther was neither of these.

"Well!" she declared crossly one day, "at least Thomas agrees with me", and flounced from the room.

I had no idea who Thomas was and became concerned that she had made an unwise acquaintance in the market. I tried to find out from her mother who the man was but she was very unforthcoming, despite both females being on the stall together.

"How do I know who she talks to?" asked Mistress Morgin impatiently. "She's one end of the trestle and I'm the other. We're both shouting our wares and keeping an eye on the goods. You'll have to ask her."

So I did, at our evening meal, for I wanted her answer to be before her parents in case of any impropriety.

"Thomas? Just a friend of mine," she replied casually. "He's a hawker. Goes round the markets, selling bits of tinware. Why?" Then she laughed. "I do believe you're jealous! Oh, that's droll! Jealous!"

I felt the colour creep up my neck and into my cheeks. No one likes to be laughed at, least of all by one's future wife. Nevertheless, I persevered. "So when do you find time to discuss the condition of women? While haggling over the price of one of his tin mugs? Or whilst he bargains with you for a foot or two of cheap lace?"

"Good gracious no! After the market's closed and mother has gone home, we dawdle about. Take a tankard of ale in a tavern, maybe, and listen to the talk. I like that. There's a lot more freedom for women nowadays. We can even talk about religion! With so many sects springing up we can pick and choose what suits us best."

"Terrible! Terrible!" exclaimed her father. "I don't hold with such thinking at all. There's no order left in life. At least with the old Church of England I knew where I was, dislike it though I did. Now it's all freedom of thought and men making out they're God's chosen saints. I don't hold with it."

"Nor with tavern going! Shameful that is!" Mistress Morgin added. "Mixing with that common lot and picking up swearwords, I dare say."

Esther laughed. "Of course! D'you want to hear a few? I've a goodly selection!"

Here I tried to intervene and recover my good standing in Esther's eyes. "Tell me about the sects you discuss. I daresay I've printed pamphlets for a goodly number of them – Baptists, Presbyterians, Arminians, Ranters, Quakers. Any number of them."

"And Diggers and Levellers, don't forget!" Esther added. "I really like the Levellers and John Lilburne's a good leader. They want to level out all social ranks – no nobles, lords or even gentry but all equal before God and the law. And all with individual liberty. A kind of republican government. All of us equal including women. And," she smiled, "I believe the Baptists even have women preachers!"

"All equal!" cried her father. "That will bring chaos! Somebody has to be at the head to give the orders. And husbands have to keep control of their families, otherwise the littlest child would make his demands and be obeyed. Chaos, as I say. Almost I would applaud the keeping of the King as head of this nation, even if only as a symbol of our subservience to God. Cromwell is becoming too powerful, from all I hear – almost like a king himself. I, for one, don't wish Charles deposed, only controlled, and his stated belief in the Divine Right of Kings done away with. A headless nation will bring chaos, I tell you."

"And what about the Diggers?" Esther challenged again. "They want to return the commons and free land to the people – no more fencing or enclosing. Just the freedom to use the land as we wish. To dig it up, if we want. Their leader, a man called Winstanley, says England belongs to the people – not to the rich. We all have rights."

After this difficult evening, relations between Esther and myself became increasingly strained. She seemed to have turned more towards this Thomas than to me. And she was right – I was very jealous of him. I feared he was usurping my position in her heart. Unfortunately my work at the printing press kept me busy until late in the evenings, for there was a constant flow of propaganda, speeches, books, cheap Bibles and religious tracts coming out that I had to see to. Many a night I walked home in the dark and fell into bed without even stopping to eat. As a consequence I was overtired and frequently short-tempered, but I was definitely making money and could see that marriage would be possible in the not too distant future. Once I was married to Esther I would have more control over her.

In the cold of January of the year 1649 we heard that the King had been beheaded in London. By March the Commons had voted to abolish the Monarchy and the House of Lords. We were now a Commonwealth and a free state, but peace did not descend on us. The Army was in dispute with the Commons, demanding voting rights for the bulk of the male population. Scotland was still unsettled – the King had, after all, been a Stuart – and there was serious trouble in Ireland, where a Royalist army was being collected to invade England.

To subdue this last threat, Cromwell ordered several regiments to sail for that island. Amongst them were the troublesome Leveller regiments but at that time Cromwell, and his general Henry Ireton, were very much out of favour with the army, so the regiments refused to serve in Ireland. A big gathering of Levellers was planned to meet in Oxfordshire and troops headed in that direction. Here, in Alton, we saw some of these men on their way through, some seeking food, ale and moral support. Then they left for Whitchurch, Andover, Newbury, Abingdon and so to the little town of Burford, where they camped overnight. Having been notified by his spies, Cromwell surrounded the mutineers while they slept and captured more than three hundred, locked them in the church for four days and then shot the leaders in the churchyard. After that the mutiny ended and Cromwell was in control again. He had declared he would break the Levellers and he had done so. I was appalled. These were members of his own army.

I no longer discussed such matters with Esther or her parents. There was no point. The relationship between Esther and the hawker continued to develop and I distrusted it more and more. The idea of women becoming independent of men seemed unnatural and not making for marital harmony. I did not like it all. Esther said I was just one of a despised old-fashioned sort, but I was not alone in feeling as I did. I had heard the phrase that our social life was turning upside down. Men were losing the command of their families while women did whatever they wished. Authority was mocked and soon even the authority of God would be disregarded. Where would we be then?

One of the pamphlets, lately published in London, was satirically entitled 'The Parliament of Women'. It described how at their imaginary meetings they voted to live in more ease, pride, pomp and wantoness, having dominance over their husbands. It was almost as if the male and female genders were being reversed – and both downgraded. Many men of my acquaintance condemned the meddling of women in politics and the beliefs of their religious sects. That they should debate, vote and even preach within their congregations seemed deplorable. If this is what freedom of political thought brought in its train, I wanted none of it – any more than had John Knox a century before when he wrote of the Monstrous Regiment of women.

In desperation and out of my continuing affection for Esther, I proposed that we should be married at once before the civil authority. She only laughed.

"I'm off with Thomas!" She declared. "We'll travel the country, living as we please, under no authority but that of ourselves! True freedom!"

I was deeply sorrowed but not surprised.

When her father was told he declared she was a wanton. "A whore – unclean and evil."

Her mother wept in real distress and shame but did, eventually, reconcile herself to the situation. It seemed Esther was not alone in her attitude – other women were living in what was once known as 'sin'. Nowadays 'sin' seemed little regarded. The world was truly topsy-turvy and her parents and I longed for a strong leader again to control these excesses and to bring back order to our lives. I'm vastly relieved to hear talk of Oliver Cromwell being made Lord Protector. I look forward to the day when this occurs. Otherwise we shall have anarchy.

Meanwhile, I continue here in Alton and now own the printing press where I worked. My left leg continues painful and increasingly shrunken, but otherwise I keep well. With my growing prosperity I feel able to look about me again for a young woman with whom to form a permanent and less troubled relationship.

Of Esther we have heard nothing. She is quite lost to us.

Based on:

"By The Sword Divided: Eyewitness Accounts of the English Civil War" by John Adair. Sutton Publishing, 1998.

"The Civil Wars, 1640-9" by Angela Anderson. Hodder & Stoughton, 1995.

"The Impact of the English Civil War" edited by John Morrill. Collins & Brown, 1991.

"The English Civil War: 1642-1651" by Philip Haythornthwaite. Arms & Armour, 1994.

"Battlefield Atlas of the English Civil War" by Anthony Baker. Ian Allan Ltd., 1986.

"Britain and the Stuarts" by D.L. Farmer. Bell & Hyman, 1965.

"The English Civil War" by Maurice Ashley. Alan Sutton, 1993.

"The World Turned Upside Down" by Christopher Hill. Penguin Books, 1975.

Booklet in the Parish Church of St Lawrence, Alton.

Display in the Curtis Museum, High Street, Alton.

James Duke of Monmouth

Chapter Ten

Fordingbridge, 1689

From his office window Richard Poole stared out at Fordingbridge High Street. Even allowing for it being market day there seemed to be more people in the town than usual. Perhaps having the new monarchs on the throne was making a difference, for Queen Mary and her Dutch husband, King William III, Prince of Orange, were both staunch Protestants and both members of the English royal family. They did seem to promise a more peaceful future and had been welcomed by a country tired of strife, whether military or religious. Some even called their Protestant accession 'the Glorious Revolution', for not a battle had been fought between the incoming Dutch and the English armies of the deposed James II. Perhaps now there would also be a cessation of troubles with France and of secret treaties with King Louis XIV. An ending, too, of the naval wars against the Dutch for the supremacy of the sea and the mercantile trade with the New World. And no more humiliations for the English such as when the Dutch admiral, De Ruyter, sailed up the River Medway in 1667 and destroyed a large number of ships at Chatham, England's premier naval base.

Turning back to his desk, the elderly Richard Poole looked at the pile of legal papers awaiting his attention. There were still too many cases to settle over inheritance; too many families to advise on their continuing efforts to regain forfeited lands lost long ago in the time of Cromwell. He sighed and was thankful old age was approaching and, before long, death. He was tired of giving advice and of sorting out confusion and unhappiness. His own life, after all, had not been overly happy. The one woman he had truly loved had now been dead for four years, brutally killed by Judge Jeffreys. Alicia Lisle had always been beyond his reach, of course, being gentry and married to gentry and somewhat older than was he. But he had loved her. And still did. He was sorely bereft by her death.

Fordingbridge, lying on the River Avon and to the west of the New Forest in Hampshire, was almost equidistant from the estates of his two most prominent clients – the Rockbourne lands of the late Sir John Cooper, which had passed to his son, Anthony Ashley Cooper, and those of the Lisles. Ashley Cooper had later set up his own home at Wimborne St. Giles in Dorset, where he had lived in considerable style in the great house built in the 1650's. The Lisles had lived in Wooton, on the

Isle of Wight but also had an estate at Moyles Court, near Ellingham, which was only a few miles south of Fordingbridge.

Richard Poole's small country practice handled very few of the Ashley Cooper affairs, for the main legal advisors were in London. Only occasionally had Richard been asked to look at some matter relating to Rockbourne, Martin, Damerham or their nearby associated hamlets. His work for Lady Alicia Lisle had consisted mostly of the collection of farm rents and the arrangement of tenancies. Thinking back to that period, he knew how foolish he must have seemed, riding over to Ellingham with his satchel full of unimportant papers in the faint hope of seeing her at Moyles. Like a love-lorn youth. And all pointless.

Their first meeting had been while her father, Sir White Beconsawe, had been still alive. As a young lad, Richard had accompanied his own father to Moyles on some minor business, and had lost his heart to her. She had been so very lovely. So smiling and gentle. When, in 1630, she had married John Lisle of Wooton and left her home to live there, he had been distraught. With the wide Solent between them, his only consolation had been the later overseeing of some of the smaller contracts for the rebuilding of the old Moyles manor house in the new, and more elegant, classical style. He was also instrumental in finding tenants to occupy it after her father's death. Smiling a little, he remembered how he had then earnestly advised against the sale of the property which had been left jointly to Alicia and her sister, Elizabeth Tipping. He had protested that the income from the rentals could prove useful to them, while being privately and desperately unwilling to lose his only contact with Alicia. And what satisfaction he had gained when Mrs. Tipping had, by a deed of 1658, relinquished her share of the Moyles estate to her sister! The chance of Richard's seeing her again increased immeasurably.

Seated in his straight-backed chair in the year 1689 – thirty years later – the elderly lawyer turned over another page of the letter his clerk had placed before him. He saw none of it. His thoughts were all of Alicia.

Despite the seeming wealth of both her own family and her husband's, he knew she had not been happy. She was John Lisle's second wife and had five children by him, one son and four daughters, but none was close to the parents. Conflict in the family was frequent for Lisle was an avid Puritan, created a viscount by Cromwell, and became the member of Parliament for Winchester and a member of the bar at Middle Temple. He was also implicated in the death of Charles I in 1649, and one of those who later nominated his master to be Protector of the Realm. As he had been living on his Isle of Wight estates at the end of the Civil war, he had been commissioned by Cromwell to take to King Charles, imprisoned in Carisbrooke Castle, the four Parliamentary Bills which would remove all royal sovereignty from him. Alicia must have been upset, although Richard had thought she was not an ardent Royalist. In fact she seemed seldom to have revealed her enthusiasms – for it was a period of such political uncertainty it was safer not to do so. He had taken great care himself to remain neutral. Clients could be of many persuasions.

Such discretion had not been followed by Alicia's son, John. He had believed strongly in the royalist cause and it was known that he despised his father for being connected with the regicides. Whether it was his father's sentencing to death of John Penruddock of Hale House, north-east of Fordingbridge, or the continuing conflicts between Alicia and her husband, Richard did not know, but it was said that the Lisle household became so unhappy that the children left home as soon as they could.

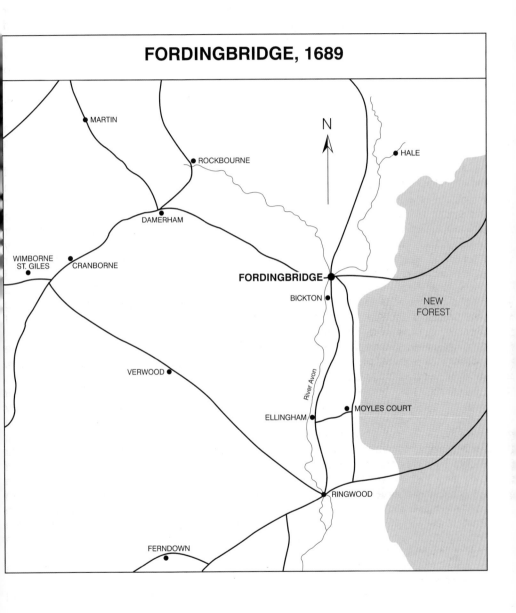

FORDINGBRIDGE, 1689

N

MARTIN

ROCKBOURNE

HALE

DAMERHAM

WIMBORNE
ST. GILES   CRANBORNE

FORDINGBRIDGE

BICKTON

NEW
FOREST

VERWOOD

River Avon

MOYLES COURT

ELLINGHAM

RINGWOOD

FERNDOWN

Young John married Catherine Croke of Dibden, on Southampton Water, according to the rites of the Church of England and in defiance of his father's Puritan ethic. He went to live at Dibden, and Richard heard later that, when drawing up his marriage settlement, he had declared he would never again live in the same house as his father. Things were no better for Alicia where her daughters were concerned. There was constant friction in the household, not least between husband and wife.

Richard sighed. The thought of what Alicia had suffered disturbed him deeply, even after this length of time. If only he could have comforted her, assured her of his admiration and devotion! With another long sigh, he picked up a small knife, intending to sharpen his quill before signing the letters. Instead he balanced it on a finger, remembering the desolation he had felt when John Lisle, seeing the imminent ending of the Commonwealth of Oliver Cromwell, had fled to Lausanne in Switzerland, dutifully accompanied by Alicia. There had been no more contact with her then. No more formal letters to be written to her at Wooton about the tenants of Moyles Court. No more equally formal letters in reply.

Later he heard that the new government of Charles II was seeking out the more virulent of his old enemies, several of whom were still in Switzerland owing to the refusal of that country to give them up. The news came, in 1664, that John Lisle had been shot by assassins. Richard Poole of Fordingbridge had rejoiced. Perhaps now the Lady Alicia would return. Perhaps now he would see her again. Perhaps now she would be happy. Life took on a new meaning. She meant all the world to him.

It was about this time that Richard acquired a small amount of work from the great Anthony Ashley Cooper who had become Lord Ashley of Wimborne St. Giles. This peerage had astounded all those who had known he had acted with Cromwell. Clearly Charles II had been a forgiving man, determined to heal the country's divisions, even between Puritans and Monarchists. Some had called him the 'Merry Monarch' because of his fondness for drink and women, plays and horseracing, yachting and dicing, but many others still had deep grievances against him. With little government finance many injustices had occurred since the Restoration. Loyal men who had gone into exile with him in 1649, thus losing their wealth and estates to the Cromwellians, naturally expected to be recompensed when he regained the throne. This did not often happen. Richard had written a dozen letters to the Exchequer on behalf of local men, beggared by their loyalty and the fines they had had to pay, and had been distressed at the paucity of replies. Now it was becoming clear that the area's more prosperous merchants, and especially those engaged in the successful cloth industry of Fordingbridge, were buying up properties from the newly impoverished landed class and setting themselves up as gentry. Some were even abandoning their often Methodist ways to become what they saw as more socially superior Anglicans and, occasionally, to occupy the previous squires' pews in church. Much mortgaging of property had also gone on, even among such local notables as John Davenant of Bickton Manor, whose family had continual financial troubles. The mortgaging and conveyancing of properties soon became the main occupation of lawyers such as Richard, to their great financial benefit but often emotional distress.

And then Anthony Ashley Cooper, Lord Ashley, that short-statured, self-important and ague-ridden turncoat, had been made Chancellor of the Exchequer when the Earl of Clarendon was removed. That he was able and astute Richard had to acknowledge, but he had also been very wealthy, partly from the ownership of extensive local landholdings and partly from successful sugar plantations in Barbados. He also had a quarter share in a ship engaged in the Guinea slave trade. He had almost too much power, even within his own sphere. Richard realized that his antipathy towards the man was underlaid by his fear that after Lord Ashley's second wife had died, he became an excellent match for the widowed Lady Lisle. She was now living in her own home of Moyles Court and this was not far away from the Ashley seat at Wimborne St. Giles. Furthermore, there was a link in their joint sympathies for the nonconformist Dissenters. Ashley had worked with the Puritans under Cromwell and must have absorbed many of their attitudes. Although he had been favoured by Charles II at the Restoration, he had argued against religious repression and the rules that disadvantaged the Presbyterians and other Dissenters, which had forced them to hold services in secret. Ashley objected to this on principle and so, Richard thought, did Lady Alicia, who had never been a keen member of the Church of England. Possibly she liked the freedom of being without bishops, of having no compulsory form of worship and of each chapel-going community being in charge of its own conventicle. It was true that she had attended the parish church of Ellingham on occasion but this could have been less for her own edification and more to reassure the villagers that Anglicanism was now fully acceptable after the Puritanism of the Commonwealth. Of Roman Catholicism no one spoke, the fear being that if King Charles failed to produce a legitimate heir his Catholic brother James, Duke of York, would come to the throne. The Dissenters as well as the Anglicans would have deplored this. And so, presumably, would the Lady Alicia Lisle and Lord Ashley. Richard became unreasoningly jealous that the two should have even this in common. He longed – as he had for so many years – for his gracious lady to turn to himself for comfort, advice and understanding and not look elsewhere.

Politically and religiously the 1670s had been a time of confusion and unrest. He remembered how he had once looked from his window on hearing shouting in the street. It had not been market noise nor drunks from the Crown Inn, but agitation. Now he tried to remember what had caused it. Fury at a new scandal caused by Charles caught in a brothel? A protest at the continuation of the Test Act, forcing every officer under the Crown to acknowledge the Anglican Church? (This was the Act that had penalised not only the Dissenters but Catholics such as James, the King's brother and heir to the throne, who had been forced to resign his position as Lord High Admiral.) Or had it been due to public horror at the King's secret treaties with Catholic France and the financial subsidies he received from Louis XIV? Or because of the lies he had told Parliament on the matter? Equally, it could have been over a resurgence of influence by the old Cabal – that association of previous leading ministers that had surrounded the King. It was true that others were now in power, such as Thomas Osborne, Earl of Danby, who was an able, industrious and clever financier who could manage both money and men. It had been said, though, that he had bribed members of Parliament to vote in favour of the King and the Anglican Church, thus creating what had become known as the Court Party. And was resented because of that bribery and the making of an increasingly upper class Church.

Richard now remembered that he had eventually distinguished some of the words shouted by those passing the open windows of his office. "Exclusion! Exclusion! Exclude the Duke of York!" Just an anti-Catholic mob, he remembered thinking, and had closed the window. The King would have to do something soon. So many people agitated for an Exclusion Bill to bar the Duke from succeeding his brother Charles. But who else had there been to take the throne? The Duke of York's Protestant daughter Mary, by his first wife, had been married to the equally Protestant William of Orange, ruler of the Dutch, and they could, Richard had supposed, become joint monarchs of England. But only if James, Duke of York, was disbarred. England was thus not at peace with itself nor with its continental neighbours. All was unrest and protest. Even Lord Ashley, who had been made Earl of Shaftesbury in 1672, was campaigning ceaselessly against the Court and the Catholic Queen as well as against the Duke of York. He had been known to raise mobs in the City of London by encouraging their cries of "No Popery!" He and his friends had gathered in coffee houses, exchanging plans and pamphlets, and plotting to gain yet more finance from the Dutch to allow their bribery to continue.

It was well-known that Shaftesbury had been fiercely opposed to the Court Party of Danby and other ex-Cavaliers, and had become undisputed leader of what came to be known as the Country Party. Richard Poole had little interest in politics, except in so far as it affected his clients, but he was shocked to hear how the King's position was weakening. Even Louise de Kéroüalle (the King's Catholic mistress who had been made the Duchess of Portsmouth with an annuity of £10,000) when threatened by Shaftesbury with proceedings against her as a common whore, quickly abandoned Charles and allied herself to his persecutor's party in self-protection. This was a serious and unkind defection, especially as at the time the King's favourite illegitimate son, the Duke of Monmouth, was also agitating against his father, desperate to be legitimized. If this had happened it would have placed Charles in the position of setting aside his own brother, James, as his legal heir – and this he refused to do, declaring such an action would be against both justice and the law of the land. The two political factions (themselves an entirely new concept) were now hurling insults at each other, the Court Party being denigrated as "Tory", which derived from an Irish word for thieves and rebels, while the Country Party was despised as the 'Whigs', from the Scots Gaelic for raiders or cattle thieves. Richard also remembered clearly the panic that had ensued when a rumoured popish plot, led by a renegade Jesuit, Titus Oates, was said to have been revealed in 1678. The Pope, it was rumoured, had ordered the Jesuits to assassinate King Charles, to put James on the throne with the help of Catholic French troops and, at the same time, to murder all London Protestants. Many people had fled that city, believing the tale.

It did not pay to be a Catholic at that time, but equally it would not have paid to have had a legitimized, though Protestant, Duke of Monmouth on the throne. As a lawyer, Richard had seen that such a legitimizing of bastardy would put the inheritance expectations of legitimate sons at risk. The great landowners now became acutely concerned about family succession, especially as the Protestant Country Party hinted that under James, as a Catholic king, landowners would have to return to the Church those abbey lands acquired at the Reformation. The King did his best to hold a balance between the factions by occasionally dissolving Parliaments, but without complete success. Finally, in 1681, he called a meeting in Oxford, which had been a consistently royalist city, and thus gained the upper hand – and with it fell the hopes of the Duke of Monmouth for formal legitimization. The Country Party also collapsed and the Whig, Anthony Ashley, now Earl of Shaftesbury, had been forced to flee the country. In January, 1683, ill and broken in spirit, he had died in the arms of his servant Wheelock, in the city of Amsterdam.

A great sense of relief had then spread throughout England, for a second civil war had been a very real possibility. Peace returned, and with it a considerable measure of ordinary prosperity. Richard's clients became less apprehensive about the future. Business expansion began again; house-building increased and social life returned to normal. Until, that is, the 6th February, 1685, when King Charles died aged 54 and his Catholic brother came to the throne as James II.

Consternation again swept the country. No one knew what to expect. Would there be persecutions of Protestants, the continued disbarring of Dissenters, restoration of Catholicism, the removal of the Church of England? Uncertainty spread through the populace and Richard was besieged by clients seeking his advice. He could give none and longed, above all else, to make certain that Lady Alicia Lisle was secure in her income and in those holdings over which he had some control. With her leanings towards the Dissenters he had feared for her future under a Catholic monarch. If only she could remain in seclusion until the situation became clearer! Moyles Court, after all, was not a large estate and he had hoped most fervently that both she and it would escape scrutiny. She had simply become an elderly lady living quietly in rural obscurity.

Real alarm had filled him, though, when he had heard that the Duke of Monmouth, who had been exiled in 1683 after his Rye House plot against his father, had returned to England. He had landed on the south coast of Dorset in Lyme Bay and had raised a rebellion against his uncle King James. Richard, along with most the country, had waited in apprehension for further news. Was there to be the dreaded civil war after all? Would the Protestants rise up behind Monmouth and fight James? Would the Whigs support the legal King, Catholic though he was, and turn their backs on a bastard son? No one had known.

In the event, the rebellious army of Dissenters and largely unarmed West Country peasants were defeated at Sedgemoor, near Bridgewater in Somerset, on the sixth of July, 1685, only two weeks after Monmouth had declared himself king in Taunton market place. It was said the defeat was largely due to the efficient artillery of the royal army, led by John Churchill, and partly to the incompetence of the rebel leaders, including the Duke of Monmouth himself. Many of the Duke's supporters ran away, leaving the dead where they had fallen. Five hundred of those captured were imprisoned in Weston church, with a score or so being hanged from its tower. Monmouth fled on horseback to the hoped-for security of Cranbourne Chase, where he and his companion Lord Grey, were said to have hidden their horses' bridles and saddlery, turning the animals loose. Despite their hiding in a dry ditch, covering themselves with bracken, they were found by troopers of Sir William Portman. Monmouth was recognized by his 'George', which he had kept in his pocket, and it was by this insignia of the Garter that the militia knew him. Imprisoned in a house in West Street, Ringwood, he had written a grovelling letter to King James, begging mercy for rebelling. That mercy had not been granted, and he along with three hundred and twenty of his supporters, had been beheaded on Tower Hill in London.

Then had begun another form of terror. The king and government settled down to the task of retribution.

Judge Jeffreys had earlier been made Lord Chancellor of England by King James, his reputation already being one of great severity and brutality. Appointed to preside over the trials of those rebels in the Western Circuit, he moved from centre to centre, conducting what were soon known as his 'bloody assizes'. There had been no leniency or pity. At Taunton he had lodged in the town while his colleague, Colonel Kirke, hanged condemned rebels from the signboard of the White Hart Inn in Fore Street. At Chard the Assize was held in the Court House and many more rebels were condemned, as they were at Salisbury, Exeter, Wells and Bristol.

Only when the Assize had reached Winchester did Richard truly quail, for Lady Alicia had been taken prisoner on a charge of siding with Monmouth. All his worst forebodings had come true. Only later had he pieced together the full story, finding that at the time of the Battle of Sedgemoor she had been in London. Surely that would exonerate her from complicity with Monmouth? But then he had worried about the reason for her trip to the capital. Why had she gone? Her married children were not there – her son John was still living at Dibden; her eldest daughter, Triphena, had fled long years before to Wales from her parents' unhappy home and was now married to her second husband, a Mr. Grove; Bridget had married Leonard Hoar from Boston in America and had returned there with him as he was shortly to become the first Principal of Harvard University. Mrs Ann Harfell, the youngest of the family, he did not know, whereas the other daughter, Margaret, lived in Fordingbridge as the wife of the Dissenting minister, Robert Whitaker, whom he knew well and for whose freedom he had long feared.

So why had Lady Lisle gone to London? With the Earl of Shaftesbury already dead in Amsterdam, it was not because of him as Richard might once have feared. The reason was unlikely to have been to do with politics as she had no strong links with either the Whigs or the Tories. And London, in July, was a severe plague risk. Richard had worried that her visit had been connected with her Dissenting beliefs and the continuing illegal use of the small Moyles Court chapel as a 'conventicle'. It was only at her trial that he learned that after her return from that strange visit to London, she had received on the 20 July, 1685, a letter from John Hickes, a Dissenting minister, asking her to shelter him. This message was carried by a man called Dunne, who had once worked for Lady Alicia as a stable boy. She had declared in Court that she had imagined this John Hickes was in trouble for no more than illegal preaching and so agreed to his request. That he was a refugee from Monmouth's army after Sedgemoor she declared she had not known. It appeared that when Hickes arrived late one evening he was accompanied by not only Dunne but by another man. This was Richard Nelthorp who was, it transpired, definitely a rebel who had also been concerned with Momouth's Rye House plot of 1683 against King Charles.

Could Alicia really be implicated in all this? Did she have a political interest in Monmouth and the rebels? Was it not more likely that she was concerned only with the man who had approached her first – John Hickes – a known nonconformist divine from Keynsham, near Bath, who in his turn might have known only of her sympathies and perhaps of her chapel? Richard's hopes were shattered when it transpired that Hickes, too, was a refugee fleeing from Sedgemoor. This made Alicia's innocence of treason for sheltering these men even more doubtful. Could she really be guilty of Judge Jefferey's charge against her?

But there had been another man in the small party that night. His name was Barter and it was he who had betrayed her and the fugitives to Colonel Penruddock of Hale House, not far away. Unhappily, it had been John Lisle, Alicia's late husband, who had sentenced to death Penruddock's royalist father in 1655 during Cromwell's Protectorate. The Colonel now sent a troop of soldiers to search Moyles Court and they found Hickes hiding in the malthouse and Nelthorp in a hole beside a chimney. If Lady Alicia was truly innocent, how did Nelthorp know the hiding place was there?

Inevitably she was arrested and taken to Winchester for trial, riding pillion behind one of the soldiers. Hickes and Nelthorp were taken to Glastonbury where, after a later trial, they were hanged, drawn and quartered. Richard had no concern for them, but for Alicia he had been desperately afraid, following her to Winchester. He had no hope of pleading for her at the trial but could not stay away. It seemed no one other than himself had seen the legal incorrectness of charging her with harbouring rebels, when those same men had not yet been convicted of rebellion. The whole trial must be an act of revenge by Colonel Penruddock for the death of his father. But when he had heard that the trial was to be before Judge Jeffreys, Richard had truly despaired. A jury had been formed but he had no faith in its impartiality, especially after he had heard that soldiers had been billeted on the townspeople to reduce them to terror for their own safety. Also Jeffreys was said to have dispensed heavy bribes to the jurymen in order to ensure Lady Lisle's conviction. Despite this, on that morning of 27 August, 1685, three times the jury declared her innocent of treason and complicity in Monmouth's insurrection. Finally, however, the Judge obtained the verdict he wished: Alicia was to burn at the stake that same afternoon.

Frantic efforts were made by loyalists and the clergy of Winchester to have her sentence reduced, but all that James II would concede was to grant a reprieve of four days and to grant her request to be beheaded rather than to burn. She was, after all, elderly, being about seventy-one years of age. So it was that on the 2nd September, Lady Alicia Lisle was beheaded in the Market Square at Winchester and her body delivered to her family for burial. As a final act of contempt, Jeffreys ordered that her head was not to be given up until the day following. Richard joined the sad cortege travelling back to Moyles but, not liking to intrude on the family, returned to Fordingbridge and his own sad house. During the following months he had spent many hours mourning her in the church of Ellingham, sickened by the thought of her head possibly lying elsewhere. He could now do nothing further, especially as her properties, confiscated by the Crown, had been granted to Lewis, Earl of Feversham. The heart had gone out of him and his legal work became no more than a duty.

Then, to the relief of multitudes, the Whigs and the Tories formed an alliance to invite Prince William, the Protestant ruler of the Dutch, and his English wife Mary, eldest daughter from the first marriage of King James, to take the throne, ruling jointly from London.

James II fled ignominiously to the continent where he continued to lay plans to muster support from the French, Scottish and, primarily, the Irish Catholics to win back his throne. But with William III and Mary ruling the country and the rebel army defeated at the Battle of the Boyne in Ireland, peace came again to England, especially since the new monarchs fully understood that they ruled only by the wishes of Parliament and no longer by Divine Right. Two of Lady Alicia's married daughters, Triphena and Bridget, applied to have the attainder reversed regarding their mother and by a private act of Parliament this was done in 1689. Richard heard the grounds for this application were that the verdict was "injuriously extorted and procured by the menaces and violences and other illegal practices" of Judge Jeffreys. Thus it was that the Moyles land was restored to the Lisles in the person of John Lisle of Dibden, son of Alicia and her husband, John. Richard Poole now had no further business connection with the family or their lands. He was old, totally dispirited, and longed for nothing so much as death. With the passing of the great love of his life he had no interest left in the world.

And so it was that on a day in 1689, he reached for the small bell on his desk. When his clerk answered its ring, he pushed the pile of letters, papers and documents across to him.

"See to these," he said sadly. "Tell my clients I am ill. I am retiring from the practice and they must find another lawyer. And you another employer. Now I shall go to my rooms and remain there. I have done with the world."

James II.   Alice de Lisle

Cromwell   Judge Jeffries

Based on:

"The Life & Times of Charles II" by Christopher Falkus. Weidenfeld & Nicolson, 1992.

"The Stuart Age: England 1603-1714" by Barry Coward. Longmans, 1994.

"Alicia Resurgam. A Brief History of Moyles Court" by Paul Hughes. 1993.

"A New History of England" by L. C. B. Seaman. Papermac, 1982.

"The Chronicle of the Royal Family". Edited by Derri Mercer. Chronicle Communications Ltd., 1991.

"Companion into Hampshire" by L. Collison-Morley. Methuen & Co. Ltd., 1948.

"A History of Hampshire" by Barbara Carpenter-Turner. Phillimore, 1978.

"The Victorian County History of Hampshire". Edited by William Page, 1908.
(Reprinted University of London Institute of Historical Research, 1973.)

"Britain and the Stuarts" by D. L. Farmer. Bell & Hyman, 1965.

Various volumes of "The Dictionary of National Biography" Edited by Sidney Lee.
Smith Elder & Co., 1894.

Leaflets from Ellingham & Rockbourne churches.

Chapter Eleven

Portsmouth, 1797

Mr. Ronaldsay Pearce was not impressed with Portsmouth. As he had explained to his wife before leaving London, he preferred establishments that were military rather than naval.

It was true there was a military garrison in the town, with the Governor as its commander, but it was not very much in evidence although its men did, of course, man the bastions, redoubts, various forts and the artillery guns. It was the Navy which was the prime reason for the town's very existence – it had never been a truly commercial port and all through the Middle Ages had been governed from Southampton.

Mr. Pearce had been given very congenial lodgings on the Grand Parade, this making it easy for him to visit the Governor's house nearby. In these circumstances he felt he could tolerate not only the Navy but the dirt, squalor and bawdiness of the old part of the town. At least, in this time of war with France, it was safer to be within the ramparts rather than outside, in the area known as Landport. Southsea, despite its castle, was much less well defended, and the whole Portsea Island was separated from the mainland only by a tidal creek and had little other protection.

He had come to Portsmouth at the behest of the Governor, who needed a solicitor and man of business to draw up the contracts for all the work being done on the old Tudor house. He had been here a matter of days only but already felt quite at home. His landlady, a Mrs. Holbrook, was very agreeable and had given him a charming bow-fronted room overlooking the Grand Parade. Her husband was the Master of a ship at present on a voyage to Australia, transporting convicts from the old hulks lying in Portsmouth Harbour.

"Sometimes I feel sorry for them" she said on one occasion, "wicked though they be. But I daresay life in Botany Bay will be better than life here. Poverty is very extreme, you know, Mr. Pearce, and it has led to a great deal of crime. Round here we suffer most severely from robberies and brutal assaults. The men are very violent and the streets are no longer safe – especially at night. It is a wicked world we live in and so I do realise the more criminals that are taken from the gaols and sent overseas the better, but I must admit to having considerable sympathy for some of them. Their crimes are often very petty."

"I agree, Mrs. Holbrook, but what else are we to do if we don't transport them? The gaols are overflowing and no longer emptied at each Quarter Session for sentences are so much longer nowadays. The old threats of fines, or whippings, or being put in the bridewell for a short time, no longer seem effective. And since the American War that country has refused to take any more of our convicts."

"It is organised gangs of wicked men we have now. Stealing animals very often, for there's always a good price for a horse." She paused for a moment and then went on, "But here in Portsmouth it's those who escape from the hulks that we fear most – not only their violence but the terrible gaol fever they bring with them. Those hulks are dirty beyond words and the men riddled with disease."

"And your husband, madam? How does he maintain his health on a convict ship and his control of all those below deck?"

"Well, since the earlier fleets went out he says conditions have definitely improved. The prisoners now have their shackles removed quite often and are thus able to inhale healthy fresh air on deck. And he has a company of soldiers to keep the discipline." She sighed heavily. "I am just so thankful he was not required to sail in the terrible Second Fleet. 1790, I believe that was. So many prisoners died it was a disgrace. From too few rations and putrid water, I understand. And the men in shackles for most of the time." She hesitated a moment and then added, "It is said that if a prisoner died, his companions in irons did not report it. That way the dead man's rations were still handed out and could be shared among the others." She lowered her gaze to her lap and whispered: "But imagine, Mr Pearce! A dead man beside you in the tropical heat! No wonder the men who did survive were sickly and useless to the Governors of this new colony."

"Madam! Please do not distress yourself!"

She smiled a little tremulously. "Indeed! I am foolish, I know, but when my thoughts are with my dear husband I do fear for his health, although conditions are so much improved."

"But he will be back soon, dear lady, and all your fears laid to rest."

She glanced at him. "But no, sir. He has been not long gone – and the voyage is near enough eight months each way, allowing time at the Cape for taking on fresh provisions as well as at Botany Bay." Then she smiled and in a more cheerful voice continued, "Let us have a cup of tea! I shall ring the bell for Clarrie and she can bring the kettle and a few little ratafia biscuits. There is no need for me to oppress you with my despondency."

During the next few days Mr Pearce spent a considerable number of hours sorting out the Governor's new building plans and contracts. Sometimes he worked in the study set aside for him in the big house on Governor's Green, next to the Garrison Church, and sometimes in his room in Mrs Holbrook's house. At other times he visited the contractors in their offices and these outings he enjoyed. Portsmouth was not as begrimed with filthy coal smoke as was London, although the town did not seem to have heeded the 'Lighting and Paving Act' of 1762 in the way that the capital had. Nor were the Scavengers as efficient – filth lay everywhere.

On his walks he would occasionally stop at a respectable-looking coffee shop, the wooden booths plain but discretely placed so that business was often carried on there. Indeed, he had many interesting conversations with local professional men and those in trade. He soon understood that Portsmouth, being a Naval town, flourished best in times of war, for then there was the spending of the sailors' prize-

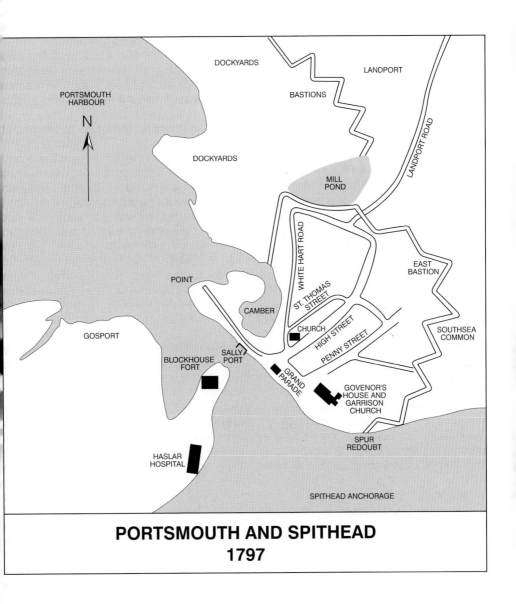

PORTSMOUTH AND SPITHEAD
1797

money from the capture of enemy vessels, and by the families of the officers now residing in the town. With the recent extension of the dockyards, there was also good custom from the manual labourers before they streamed home through the various rampart gates to their recently built houses on old Portsea Common.

Sometimes he would eat his evening meal in a chop house, frequently in the High Street, although he deplored having to avoid the filth outside the public houses where the gutters were used as latrines by the populace – used, he found, quite blatantly and without discretion. The smell was very offensive and the streets hazardous. Some of the worst offenders in this respect were the poor who rented single rooms in the upper storeys of houses, for they simply emptied their dirty water and effluent out of the windows. This was, of course, against the law and the culprit could be turned over to the Constable, but few ever were.

On one such evening, as he picked his way along the main thoroughfare and turned into St Thomas Street, he collided with a man lurching towards him. They both stumbled, Mr Pearce clutching the other for support. He found the stranger's clothing soaking wet. Apprehensive that he held an escaped convict from a prison ship, he feared for his life. Stabbed bodies were nothing new in Portsmouth.

"Sorry, sir," the man panted. "Didn't see you." Weakly, he tried to pull away but the solicitor held him tightly.

"You're wet! Swam from one of the hulks, did you?"

"No, sir. But the Press Gang was after me – for the Navy, like – so I ran. Then I slipped off the harbour wall and into the water. Please let me go, sir. I must get back to my family."

Mr. Pearce did not know whether to believe him or not but he let him go nevertheless. Then he turned and went on his way, but very alert for the sound of footsteps running behind him and of the threat of a knife in his back. When he reached the street corner he glanced back. The man was where he had left him, leaning against the wall. He had not seemed like a rogue nor an escaped convict. More like an exhausted countryman, very scared of capture by the Press Gang and of being forced into the Navy.

Slowly the lawyer walked back. This appeared to be a case of genuine need. The man had not been captured, after all, for he wore neither handcuffs nor shackles. He was free and wished to remain so. Mr. Pearce made up his mind.

"I have rooms near here," he said. "Come back with me and at least get warm again. The Press men won't take you if we are together – I'm working for the Governor."

The man nodded but did not speak. Slowly they walked side by side back to Grand Parade and his lodgings. When Clarrie let them in, he asked for his landlady.

"Mrs Holbrook, may I beg your indulgence? I wish to take this young man to my room as he has fallen into the Harbour and is very cold. I can lend him a coat of my own while his clothes dry a little, but I would be deeply grateful if Clarrie could supply us with a little warming tea."

"Oh, Mr Pearce, do you really think – I mean, those that fall in the Harbour are usually – oh dear. Well, as you wish. Clarrie will bring up the tea and place the wet clothing near the kitchen fire."

He bowed to her and led the shivering refugee up the stairs to his room. "Now, strip," he commanded. "Leave your wet clothes there and I will find you some covering."

When the man was decent again he sat him down by the fire and, after Clarrie's discreet knock, plied him with hot tea. "Now your name, if you please."

"Jonathan Fitch. Of Wymering." He looked up pleadingly. "I'm not a criminal! I swear not! Just chased by the Press. I work at Manor Farm and never done nothing wrong. I was only in Portsmouth to see my cousin. Then those Navy Board men tried to grab me. And I've a wife and children, sir. Can't leave them, sir. Nor my job, for if I'm not working they'll be thrown out of the cottage and another man put int."

"There's a war on, Fitch, and the Navy needs men. If they won't volunteer, how are they to be found?"

The man hesitated a moment, clearly not sure if he could answer truthfully. Then he said slowly. "By paying them more, sir, and treating them proper. My cousin's a seaman and he says conditions are cruel. Near to starvation some of the crews are – seems the Pursers take most of the money due for rations and then set themselves up in style."

"Perhaps the country can't afford to pay the seamen more. Have you thought of that? Taxation is already higher than I have ever known it but still the money is short. There has been a run on the Bank of England as well – everyone of consequence is trying to convert paper money into coin for hoarding. Paper notes will soon be so much waste paper. And it is not just the Navy expenditure – what about the Army? Apparently there is a new French general who is a real threat to us. Napoleon Bonaparte, I believe his name is. We have to defeat the French somehow. It all takes money."

"Indeed, sir. But you won't get the best service out of pressed men who are treated bad. Makes them resentful, see. They're patriotic, sir, same as you and me, but they need to be paid – and not as now, sometimes two years or more in arrears, but when it's due. And another thing, sir, the rate they get is the same as more than fifty years ago. With everything costing more now, pay doesn't go far. It really doesn't."

Mr Pearce thought of the estimates for building work he had given the Governor. They far exceeded the sum expected. Construction costs were rising fast because the population of the port was increasing markedly owing to Naval expansion. All the extra dockyard workers and their families needed housing, and as the supply of craftsmen proved insufficient, so costs rose. Supply and demand, he thought ruefully, supply and demand. And as the supply dwindled, so costs rose. "We all have to tighten our belts, Fitch, unless we want to be conquered by the French."

"None of us wants that, sir. Course not. But my cousin says when a ship's in port there's no shore-leave. So he can't see his wife and babies. And that's cruel, sir."

"There's no shore-leave because of fear of desertions. How many seamen would report back to their ships if they were allowed ashore? Eh? Not many, I guess, if the ship was in its home port."

"And home ports, sir, that's another complaint. If a man is discharged from one ship in, say, Portsmouth, but had joined that ship at her home port of Plymouth, then he's not given his due money – only tokens. These he has to take all the way to Plymouth to exchange for coins. How's he to live between whiles, sir? It's a mighty long walk from here to Plymouth. And his family has been without that pay for perhaps years and had to go on the parish Poor Rates – which none of them wants. The only way is for a discharged man to sell the tokens to the bumboat women who go alongside – and who usually cheat them."

When the man stopped speaking Mr Pearce was at a loss as to how to comment. He cleared his throat. "Well, Fitch, it seems the Navy is in need of reform. When the war is over perhaps it will be seen to."

Fitch shook his head. "It'll be too late, sir. We won't have a Navy by then. Look at all the mutinies we've already had – there were four, I think, here in Portsmouth in the 1780's, and we've already had five in the '90's. And it's not just the Navy – I heard of an Army regiment (from Scotland, it was) who refused to embark for the West Indies. They'd had no pay either, and something like three hundred of them got ashore and set off north. They was recaptured at Fareham, though, and brought back. It was the Mayor of Portsmouth what eased the trouble. Sir John Carter, that was. He wouldn't let the authorities flog nor hang those soldiers, and when the famous admiral, Lord Howe, came down from London he quieted the situation. A great man he is, sir, and ever popular with us all. 'Black Dick' we calls him, on account of his dark complexion. Once he even stopped a lot of sailors threatening to run their ships ashore in the Solent if they didn't get their pay. A fine man, sir. Him, and Admiral Collingwood. The best we've got."

Mr Pearce threw a few pieces of coal on the fire. "I was in London that year. 1783, I think it was. A party of seamen marched up to London to present a petition to King George, but of what it consisted I am not sure."

"All I know," Fitch intervened, "is that the Admiral Howe obtained the pay, and whole companies from three of the great ships at Spithead came ashore with colours flying and bands playing. All the town rejoiced, sir, for everyone had been following reports in the local press and were nearly all on the side of the men over pay."

"But not all, I seem to remember. During the American War I believe there were spies and saboteurs here – and fire raisers. Was there not one nicknamed 'Jack the Painter' who planned to set fire to all the British dockyards?"

"Yes, sir. But he was caught, sir. After setting fire to the Rope House. Seems he'd been in America and liked their republican ways. He was tried for treason in Winchester and hanged near the dockyard gates here, at the top of the sixty-four feet high mizzenmast of the 'Arethusa', erected special. I heard that later his body was taken to Blockhouse Fort – that's the other side of the Harbour – and hung in chains for all to see. As bits of the skeleton fell down, the sailors would take a bone or two and pay their alehouse debts with them. Worth a bit, those bones were. Everyone wanted them."

"And the French Revolution – did that affect the people in the same way as in France? Turn people against the King?"

"Not that I've heard, sir. But then we English don't side much with the French, do we? Especially since they're now allies with the American rebels, along with the Spanish. It's not the working men who agrees with these new French ideas – only some of the clever ones. The book-learned, and that. And I don't suppose many of them. My cousin says the officers are all for King and country. Patriotic." He shifted his position a little and added, "Even if some take their duty too far. Real cruel, they can be. Too many floggings."

Mr Pearce glanced at him sharply to show the man he could not approve of criticising officers. "But mostly, sir," he added in a conciliatory tone of voice, "the cruel ones are only jumped-up men. Not used to Navy ways. Or to seamen. Being officers goes to their heads, like, and they don't use their positions as they should. Become brutal."

The older man stood up. The conversation had gone far enough. "Well, Fitch, I think your clothes should be dryer by now and you should get off home." He rang the bell and asked Clarrie to bring the man's garments and show him back to the room where he could change. Then they walked together the short distance to the High Street where they separated, Fitch effusive in his thanks.

On a fine Sunday afternoon, having attended Divine Service in the Royal Garrison Church and watched the military parade from his own window afterwards, he thought he would wander down to Point. This small peninsular, being outside the defensive fortifications and thus the jurisdiction of the city authorities, was a crowded and disorganised area. Here, as he soon discovered, the inhabitants were both rough and largely disreputable. He was glad he had left his silver-topped cane behind and had the foresight to change from his Sunday finery to less showy clothing. At every step he feared a mugging and had to remain alert to avoid drunken men who spilled from the taverns. As he walked down Broad Street, he gazed at the litter-covered mud of the Camber, went past the Town Quay and out again to the waterfront, having counted more than two dozen drinking dens. Outside 'The Still' (so named, he believed, after a particular whistle on a bosun's pipe) he saw ruffians who were probably smugglers as well as fishermen and, of course, sailors from merchant ships anchored off shore having traded, perhaps, with the spice islands of the East Indies or with South America. He enjoyed watching all that was going on while listening to the creaking inn signs and the constant tapping sounds of the rigging on the smaller boats. All very different from London. In the quieter streets, nearer the ramparts, he found a weather-boarded house overhanging the water. On enquiry he found this was Quebec House, built by public subscription in 1754 for sea-water bathing. Looking at the filth in the water, he shuddered at the thought of immersion here.

The next day he left by coach for London, and was pleased that he had been able to obtain an inside seat, for the spring weather was still cold and blustery. Before leaving his pleasant lodgings he had asked Mrs Holbrook if he could return in a few weeks time, after he had completed the work awaiting him in his London office. He told her he was very happy to pay a retaining fee for the room.

"No, no! My dear sir! I have very few applications for rooms at this time of year and, with your connections with the Governor, I can do no less than keep your room until your happy return."

So it was arranged, and he returned to his own home in Hackney Wick and his office in the City. His wife and two children were delighted to see him and he was soon absorbed in his normal life. From then on, however, he did pay particular attention to reports in The Times which mentioned the Navy and, in particular, Portsmouth. He was especially concerned when he read in early April that there was a renewed threat of serious mutiny there. It seemed that seamen of the various ships anchored at Spithead had a secret organisation, led by Valentine Joyce, a quartermaster's young mate. Getting no satisfaction for their very real complaints, they had sent a petition to old Lord Howe, although he had now retired from the Navy and was in Bath. He had then taken it to London and laid it before Lord Spencer, the First Lord of the Admiralty. Nothing came of this, however, so after a month and when the ships were again at Spithead, the men refused an order to put to sea unless they had some redress. Lower-deck informers reported that the men held almost daily meetings, with papers and secret arrangements being passed from ship to ship. The situation was becoming serious.

On the fourteenth of April, Mr Pearce read that Captain Patton, the transport officer at Portsmouth, was aboard the 'Queen Charlotte' and found groups of crew members in deep and angry discussion. Sensing something very wrong, he hurried ashore to send a message to the Admiralty by the new telegraph system installed on Southsea beach. There, by means of semaphore arms, which were seen by other stations in turn (the first being on Portsdown Hill) the message was passed across the country to the roof of Admiralty House. Patton's message read: "Mutiny brewing at Spithead", and was seen in London not many minutes later.

Orders were received in Portsmouth by Lord Bridport, the Commander in Chief of the Channel Fleet, on the sixteenth. His ships were to put to sea but, when these orders were passed on, the crews refused to sail. The men's delegates were polite but insistent that their demands should first be met.

In London the whole matter appeared very confused, for riders were said to be galloping to and fro with new orders, new offers of money and new amendments to those offers. Threats had been issued to the men but without effect. It seemed they wanted their grievances dealt with, particularly with regard to pay, better rations and the elimination of brutal treatment by certain officers. Another demand was to have an Act passed by Parliament giving them indemnity against future punishment for present behaviour. Apparently negotiations continued on board the various ships between the men's council and the admirals, and all might have gone well if Valentine Joyce had not decided to call another meeting aboard his own ship, the 'Royal George'. The signal for this was the hoisting of a red flag. Unfortunately, this was also the normal signal flown when a ship was going into action. The Times reported that not only the officers on board but the crowds of anxious people on shore took this to mean the start of a bloody revolution, especially when it was seen that the guns had now been mounted by the mutineers.

"I must return to Portsmouth," Mr Pearce declared, after reading of this. "I am concerned for Mrs Holbrook and her servant girl. With her husband at sea and her house vulnerable to attack, she will be very nervous. I think I must go." Then he added, "Besides, if there's fighting on land, the Governor's house is sure to be assailed and I have left there all my plans for the alterations. I do not wish them lost."

He saw his wife smile. She knew how he liked to be in the thick of any drama.

Thus it was that two days later Mr Pearce knocked on the door of the house in Grand Parade and was let in by a scared Clarrie.

"Oh, sir! I'm that glad to see you back, sir. Madam has been so worried. We can see the ships from the top windows with a spyglass. That red flag, and all."

Mrs Holbrook came from the sitting room. "Now we are safe, Clarrie! With Mr Pearce here we will be quite safe. How are you, my dear sir?"

"Well! Well! And I have brought my pistol with me. But how are you?"

Over the evening meal – which he vowed to eat with her every night until the emergency was over – he caught up with the latest news. He was told that at one point the red flag had come down and that of Admiral Bridport hoisted in its place. The other ships had kept theirs flying, however, as not all the rebels believed that Parliament had truly granted their demands. Luckily the Admiral could reassure them on this as he held the original proclamation, bearing the stamp of the King's own seal upon it. After that all were satisfied and the remaining red flags were hauled down. Peace seemed to have arrived. The populace, like the mutineers, greeted this with joy and cheering.

"But," Mrs Holbrook added, "things are not ended, after all. Firstly, we have suffered a most terrible gale, preventing Admiral Bridport from taking the fleet to sea as ordered. Then we heard the men's pay had not arrived as it was meant to. Now the seamen feel they have been betrayed. Especially as the marines on board have been ordered to check their arms and ammunition. The sailors, of course, saw this and feared the worst. So a second mutiny has now broken out. Oh, Mr Pearce! I really fear for our lives! Those men – what will they do when they come ashore as they surely will?"

"Are the red flags run up again?"

"Oh, yes! And the ships at the St. Helen's anchorage sent up such a cheer. They must be really blood-thirsty by now and no longer open to reason. And, Mr Pearce, today I saw several officers rowed ashore here, as if forced to leave their various ships, for there was no ceremony over their landing. Next we saw most of the Spithead vessels moved out to St. Helen's to join the others. Someone in the street said that there they would be out of range of the Portsmouth guns and could flee if other ships were sent to subdue them."

"But nothing is happening now?"

"No, I think not. But perhaps we could climb to the top floor again and use the spyglass?"

This is what they did and to their consternation saw much activity on board the 'London', still moored at Spithead. Even from that distance they could hear several shots fired and a great anxiety fell upon them.

"Clarrie," Mr Pearce said to the maid, who had followed them upstairs, "make sure the doors are locked and chained, and the windows well-shuttered."

"Yes, sir. Indeed, sir. I'll fasten them all."

It was not until the next day that they heard what had occurred. Apparently, some men had been confined below deck on the 'London' by Vice-Admiral Colpoy, and when they forced open the hatch covers and emerged they were fired on by officers, including a Lieutenant Bover. Some seamen had small arms and fired back. Several men were wounded on both sides so the mutineers locked Colpoys and two other officers in their cabins. All the other officers were sent ashore. The wounded men were taken to Haslar Hospital, on the Gosport side of the Solent, where three died.

When Mr Pearce ventured out to gather what further news he could, he heard there was now a dispute with the Military authorities. The delegates, appointed by the seamen, had demanded a proper funeral procession to be allowed to march from Haslar through Portsmouth to the Kingston churchyard for the burials. But the Garrison was now on a war footing and had manned the fortifications, raised the drawbridges over the various moats and even prepared the guns of the shore batteries. They had no wish to let the enemy within the walls, even to carry coffins.

When he returned to Grand Parade, Mr Pearce was able to tell Mrs Holbrook that it was the mayor, Sir John Carter, who had saved the situation. He had suggested that, instead of travelling round by road on a provocative route, the coffins should be rowed across the Harbour. A party of fifty men from the 'London' could then march behind them to Kingston for burial. Mr. Pearce then went out to join the crowds lining the route. He liked to feel a part of things.

Apparently the news of the second mutiny had hurried up affairs in London, for the 'Seamen's Bill' was quickly passed by Parliament. The fate of the three officers, still prisoners on board 'London', was as yet undecided but when the men saw a copy of the resolution about increased pay, they released Colpoys and one other, but not Bover because it was he who had killed a shipmate of theirs. However, as all three officers had to attend the Coroner's Court about this death, they agreed to release Bover as well, on condition that he gave his word to return as their prisoner. And return he did, even though the verdict had been 'justifiable homicide' and he was thus legally free. When he was once again on 'London', the crew greeted him with three cheers for being an honourable man and gave him back his liberty. He was even asked to continue to serve with the ship, and this he said he would do.

"A truly honourable man," as Mrs Holbrook said.

Mr Pearce now had to attend to the last of his business at the Governor's house, and it was there that he heard that the venerable Lord Howe was to come to Portsmouth. The old man, being revered by the Navy, had been asked by the Cabinet to explain the new position to the men and to quieten any remaining resentments. He came, with his wife, and stayed with the Governor, determined to do what he could, despite acute pain from an attack of gout.

That same day, 10th May, as well as on the following two, he was taken by barge to all the ships in turn, talking to each ship's company on the quarter-deck. Although at first he refused all help up and down the ships' ladders, by the end he had to be lifted in and out of his boat. On the fourth day he held long discussions with the delegates about the removal of unpopular officers. Finally it was agreed that fifty-nine of them should be removed and this the Admiralty confirmed by telegraph.

Just as it seemed all was settled, eight ships from Plymouth sailed into Spithead flying the red flag of revolt. At once Howe went on board their flagship and talked to the men, finally agreeing to the removal of a further sixty-five officers and warrant officers. The red symbol was hauled down and another mutiny was thus averted.

The next day Howe was escorted ashore by a procession of boats after his final visit to the 'Royal William'. When he landed at Point he was cheered continuously by an enormous crowd, then he and Lady Howe walked together to the Governor's house. Mr Pearce and his landlady watched the crowds from the sitting room window, but they only heard later about the next gratifying incident. It seemed that Valentine Joyce, the leading mutineer, stepped forward and spoke very respectfully to the old admiral, enquiring at what time he would embark on the following day for the formal reconciliation with the delegates aboard the 'Royal William'. When the time was arranged, Howe asked Joyce to join him inside and have a glass of wine. This he did.

The next day the crowds were out early, including Mr Pearce and his landlady, and there was much jostling for places. In due course, a procession of naval boats appeared in the harbour, the leading one flying the Union Jack, and containing the men's delegates. They all landed at the Sally Port and marched to the Governor's house, led by a band playing lustily. Lord Howe invited the delegates into the house to drink wine with him and then took them onto the balcony to wave to the crowd, which responded with thunderous applause. On returning to the Sally Port, they embarked in the procession of boats (with Lord Howe carrying the royal pardon and indemnity) and took him to every ship. At six o'clock the boats came back to the Sally Port but by this time Lord Howe was so exhausted that he had to be lifted from the barge. The same seamen then carried him on their shoulders back to the Governor's house, through the cheering crowds and the near deafening noise of the firing of the military guns in salute. Late that night the delegates returned by moonlight to their ships and the mutiny was over.

The next morning Mr Pearce retrieved the last of his belongings from the Governor's house, packed his own bags and said goodbye to Mrs Holbrook.

"Dear Mr Pearce," she murmured. "It has been so very great a pleasure to have you here. I can only hope you will come again."

"Be assured of that," he replied. "I shall not forget my stay here. We have seen such momentous events. And seen them together."

Then he reached for her hand and, bending, kissed it gently, "Dear lady." Then he smiled at her, gathered up his bags, pressed a few coins into Clarrie's hand and went out into Grand Parade to make his way to the London coach.

Based on:

"The Naval Mutiny at Spithead, 1797" by A. Temple Patterson. Portsmouth Papers, No.5, 1968.

"Portsmouth During the Great French Wars, 1770-1880" by Alastair Gedder. Portsmouth Papers, No.9, 1970.

"Life in a Georgian City" by Dan Quickshank & Neil Burton. Viking, 1990.

"Hampshire & Australia, 1783-1791" by Margaret Spence. Hampshire Papers, No.2, 1992.

"The Buildings of Hampshire and the Isle of Wight" by Nikolaus Pevsner & David Lloyd. Penguin Books, 1985.

"Portsmouth & Environs" by George James Rogers. 1980.

"The Semaphore: the story of the Admiralty to Portsmouth Telegraph" by T.W. Holmes. Stockwell, 1983.

Maps & Photocopies of Old Portsmouth from Portsmouth City Museum.

Chapter Twelve

Andover, 1830 and 1846

"**C**ome on, son! The fight's beginning!" Matthew Dodds picked up his wooden bludgeon and strode into the street.

Excited, Joseph followed. He was eleven years old and thus nearly a man. For this was mens' work and his younger brothers had to stay at home. He was very proud to be with his father in this fight for justice – had not the family been starving for long enough? Been hungry day and night, with the little ones whimpering because of their empty bellies? Now it was time to put things to rights and demand higher wages for his father. To do this, it seemed, they were going to have to smash the new-fangled machinery that was putting men out of work. Evil, they were, his father said. All over the south country there were riots, led by a Captain Swing, and they were usually against machinery.

But fires had been laid, too, burning down corn ricks; farmers threatened if they did not raise their men's money; threshing machines smashed – particularly the threshing machines. Until those mechanical brutes arrived on the farms, country folk lived all winter by earnings from flail-threshing the corn in the dry of the barns. Now the machines did it all in two weeks or so and the men, having no work, were turned off. Joseph knew there was Outdoor Relief from the parish rates but it was never enough. And recently the price of bread had gone up again. Hunger was all about.

Grasping his stick more firmly he followed his father into the town. It was Saturday morning and he should have been at work in the brewer's yard, tending the big dray horses. But today was special. Today there was to be a riot and he was counted as a man.

As they hurried through the streets they were joined by dozens of labourers, carrying axes, hammers or other tools. He had never seen so many men – except at the great autumn fair on Weyhill Down – and these men were all angry. Fierce, they looked, and he hurried to keep pace with his father.

In front of the Angel Hotel they all stopped. "There's magistrates in there," someone said. "Three of them. Holding a meeting."

This was greeted with a growl from the mob, but when an upper window was opened and one of the legal men appeared, silence fell. In a loud voice he began to read from a paper. This was the Riot Act, it seemed. Then the window was shut again and the crowd broke into noisy shouting. Two men from the front of the mob pushed into the hotel. Ringleaders, Joseph thought they must be. Others tried to enter, too. John Gilmore, a labourer from Upper Clatford who was well known in the town, set his back against the door and shouted: "There's enough in already. Come back later."

After a while the crowd dispersed, roaming the town but not causing trouble. A rumour spread among them that an attack was planned against the printing works of John Bensley. There was more new machinery there, it seemed. But then it was heard that the attack was called off as beer money had been paid and the works were to be left alone.

"We're to smash Tasker's Iron Foundry instead. Up Clatford Marsh way, in the Anna Valley."

Joseph clutched his weapon more tightly and looked as fierce as he could. Then he asked, "Now? Can we go now?"

"No, lad. We gather this afternoon. Armed with bludgeons."

By the time the mob left Andover at about three o'clock, Joseph had lost sight of his father. He was not concerned about this for all were going the one way. Avoiding the Salisbury turnpike and taking the smaller roads to the south, they headed for the bridge over the River Anton. There they all stopped while the ironwork on the bridge was destroyed.

"Why?" Joseph wanted to know. "That's not machinery! Why are we smashing it?"

"'Cos it's made by Tasker's, see. Who makes machinery what puts us out of work. That's why we're going to the Foundry. So no more iron machinery can get made there."

Joseph nodded. Later the order came down the lane to form into columns of three, and this they did, with much shuffling and confusion. "Like blooming soldiers!" someone grumbled. The three leaders were James and Isaac Mann, brothers, and between them was Charles Fay, who carried a flag in one hand and a pickaxe in the other. When the Foundry came in sight it was realized that the great gates were shut and no smoke came from the fire in the cupola. The furnace had obviously been drawn much earlier and was now probably cold.

Two men stood just outside the gates but Joseph, being small and unable to see, edged his way through the crowd to near the front. One of the two men he guessed to be Robert Tasker, the owner, and the other a foreman of some sort. Both were attempting to dissuade the mob from entering the Foundry yard. Tasker was offering £100 if the men would go away.

"We're not going!" a voice shouted. "The Foundry's ruining us. Making that machinery! Taking our jobs from us, it is. Carpenters, wheelwrights, weavers – all of us. And the land labourers – they're the worst off. All them threshing machines – took the place of the flail, they have, and now our families 'll be out of work all winter. And it's end of November now."

Cries of agreement went up from the men. "Smash the machines! Smash 'em! Smash 'em!"

Joseph could see Mr. Tasker speaking to the Mann brothers, obviously pleading. Isaac nodded before turning to James. Whatever agreement they were coming to was overturned by the mob at their rear, some of whom shouted to go

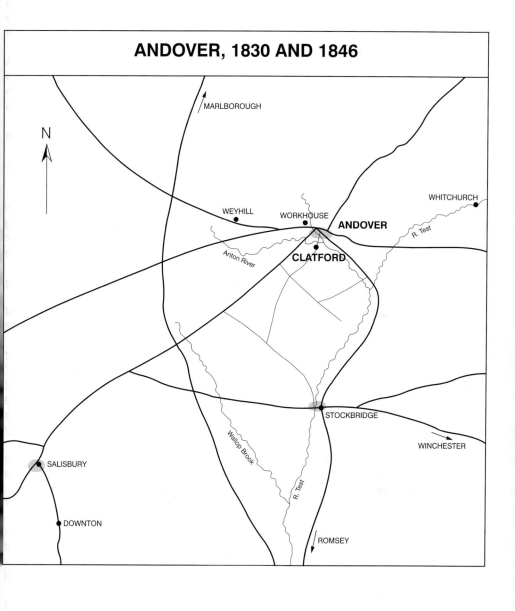

ANDOVER, 1830 AND 1846

N

MARLBOROUGH

WHITCHURCH

WEYHILL

WORKHOUSE

ANDOVER

R. Test

Anton River

CLATFORD

STOCKBRIDGE

WINCHESTER

Wallop Brook

SALISBURY

R. Test

DOWNTON

ROMSEY

on. Others began to shake the gates. Isaac hesitated a moment and then thrust the foreman aside.

"Let me come to the lock," he demanded. Raising his heavy, iron-tipped bludgeon, he brought it down on the padlock and struck it off with the one blow.

The gates swung open and the men poured across the yard and into the moulding shop. Joseph was swept along, too, but did not enter the building, from which now came sounds of blows of metal on metal, accompanied by much shouting and cheers. Then there was a crash of glass and an iron handle, apparently from a mould-box, flew through a window and fell into the yard. Others followed. Tasker's foreman shouted to those outside to stand clear, for otherwise they would have their brains knocked out by those inside. Most moved back a little, Joseph included. He saw one man, John Ellis, standing by himself, shaking his head. The foreman went up to him and asked, "Can't you stop it? Those handles are wrought iron and not cast at all. You've no reason to fear hand-made things – only the machine-made."

Ellis shrugged his shoulders, but going closer to the building he cupped his hands and cried, "Ahoy! Ahoy!"

Inside, the hammering and the shouting stopped and Ellis announced that they would be given any money they liked if they ended the destruction. There was a brief silence and then one of the leaders shouted back, "Damn their eyes! We won't take their money! Go back to work, boys!"

So the smashing and the hammering resumed and then grew louder, for the men had now found the work's own sledgehammers and other heavy tools. Joseph became frightened. The riot was no longer exciting. With every window smashed, men were now tearing off the roof. They were throwing down the chimney and smashing the walls. One man ran to the Foundry crane and smashed its cast-iron gearing. Another attacked the lathe. Even half-made iron implements were destroyed, including ploughs and rollers, neither of which put labourers out of work. Others looked round for threshing machines but, as Tasker's did not make them, they ran for the waterwheel which powered much of the Foundry. They knocked off the floats, smashed the hatches controlling the flow of water, bent and made useless the cast-iron paddles.

Joseph wished to go home but by now the November sky was dark and he felt safer among the crowd. Cold and miserable, he sheltered near a store shed while the destruction went on for several hours. Then, quite suddenly, the noise stopped. The men dropped their tools and began to stream away.

"Are we going now?" he asked hopefully.

"Aye, lad. It's near midnight so it'll be Sunday soon. We don't do fighting on a holy day so we're off home. Back on Monday, though."

The boy followed the crowd through the lanes for the two miles back to Andover. He was very weary and not as exhilarated as he felt he should be. The uncontrolled violence of the mob had scared him. When his father returned home even later, he announced he would join those returning to the Foundry on the Monday morning. Nervously Joseph offered to accompany him, although he would have preferred to go to work as usual. Being with the brewery dray horses was safer.

In the early light of the Monday morning, a small group of determined men left for the Foundry, Joseph among them. He did not wish to appear a coward before his father.

They arrived at the Foundry gates and cautiously pushed their way in, seeking new targets to attack. They moved quietly and without shouting and were thus all the more shocked when a loud voice commanded them to halt. Startled, they saw they were surrounded by soldiers and caught in an ambush. Some of the men managed to flee but others were held fast, Joseph's father among them. Truly scared, the boy ran for the gates and escaped through them as they were slammed shut, although one solider made a grab at him, tearing his coat sleeve.

He ran through the lanes, uncertain of his way in the chill light of dawn. Eventually he came to a field gate and, climbing over it, collapsed on the grass behind the hedge. As his breath returned, he realized he could not go home. His father was a prisoner and would go to jail. Or even be shipped overseas, as criminals were, or – terrible thought – hanged. He himself could be identified by the soldier who had grabbed him, and be marked out as a rioter. He would count as a criminal from now on.

After a while he climbed back to the lane and set off in the direction of Salisbury. He might be safe in a big town, especially as it was in another county and the authorities would be different. By the time he reached the Wallop Brook he was not only tired but hungry. He drank from the stream and then sat down to rest. To his dismay he became aware of a troop of mounted soldiers trotting along the side of the hill. Filled with fear again, he shrank behind a bush and stayed very still. Only when they had been out of sight for some time did he return to the road and struggle on. After a while another road came in from his left and this carried more traffic. Perhaps he could beg a lift on one of the farm carts rumbling by. With this in mind, he stood beside the road and hoped he looked as helpless as he felt. To his delight a cart containing five pigs did stop and he was invited to join the farmer on the frontboard.

When they reached the city, Joseph delivered his thanks and slipped away to look for food and a job. He had no money, no references and knew nobody in the locality. After stealing a pie from a stall and wandering the streets for hours, asking for work without success, he began to despair. Finally he was taken on as a drover's boy by a shepherd taking sheep to a farm in Downton. There, in payment, he was fed, allowed to sleep in the barn and the next day set on his way for Ringwood. When he left that town he was still without work. It seemed that times were as hard there as they had been at home and very little casual work was needed. Not only had harvests been bad, but commerce had not recovered from the long decline since the French wars had ended. Moreover, trade with the independent states of America had been very difficult after their war against England in 1812. Joseph did not understand the reasons for any of this, but from hearing his parents talking he knew that real hardship lay over England and that famine was not far off. He began to fear for himself. He was very hungry again.

Setting off for the town of Poole to the south, he hoped the port was as thriving and busy as he had been told it was. Perhaps unemployment had not hit as hard there as inland.

After only a few hours in the town (which he had spent mostly in gazing at ships and the sea, none of which he had seen before) he was at last offered work. He was taken on as a horseboy in the stables of The King Charles, one of the leading inns. With good food from the kitchen and a warm bed in the hay, he was very content. In fact, he stayed in the same job all that December of 1830 and on into the spring and the following summer.

In the autumn the landlord discovered he could read and write. "My mother taught me," Joseph told him. "We weren't always poor and on Parish Relief. My father was a handloom weaver with two apprentices and a journeyman under him." He went on to explain that when machinery came in much of the cloth industry moved to the north. "To Bradford and such. And by then there were fewer sheep, for the wool-pastures had all been ploughed up for corn during the wars. So customers didn't want our cloth – too slow in the hand weaving and so cost too much. Our journeyman had to be dismissed and no more apprentices taken on. I was going to be an apprentice, too", he added. "But my father said there was no point. I'd do better in an office, apprenticed to be a clerk. Only nobody wanted me and we'd no money for the indentures."

Joseph was careful to mention nothing abut the riot at Tasker's Foundry, nor that his father was either in prison, hanged or transported. That was too risky to be revealed. When he was asked why he was so far from home, he explained there was no work in Andover and that he had arrived in Poole more or less by chance. "I'd heard it was a great and busy port," he added.

"Used to be!" the landlord told him. "Now it's all run down. There are only the oysterbeds and the quarrying of white ball-clay for the pottery to keep us going."

Two days later he offered Joseph a job in the office of the inn. "You're young but a good worker. I think you could manage it. Doing accounts and such. Dealing with brewery orders and booking in customers. I can't give you big pay but it'll be more than I'm giving you now."

So Joseph ceased to be a horseboy and became a clerk, as his father had intended. He remained in that position for fifteen years, daily gaining in experience and seeing a gradual revival of the old port as business picked up after the depression. He also acquired a wife. Hannah and he were able to rent one of the new cottages going up on the outskirts of the expanding town. There they brought up their two children and began to prosper.

It was only in 1846 that Joseph felt secure enough to be able to face the past and to shed his deep fear of being recognised as a rioter. He begged time off from his employer, left Hannah with a small pile of coins and set off for Andover on a hired horse. There, as he rode through the streets, he recognized nobody and so grew confident that nobody would recognize him – after all, he had been away for over fifteen years and grown to manhood in that time. He began to search for his family's house but never found it, for there were new buildings and shops in its place.

When a woman approached he asked if she knew where the Dodds family had gone. "They were here in 1830, but William Dodds was taken by the soldiers in the riot at Tasker's Foundry."

"Oh, those Dodds! Well, he's dead. Died in prison. Sarah Dodds and three of her kiddies got put in the new Union Workhouse. Moved forcible from the old Poor House when the new rules came in. 1834, or thereabouts, that was. The children died – starvation, as I heard – but she's still in there. Old now, though. I only know 'cos my sister, Lottie Alder, and her four young 'uns got put in there, too. Class Six, they'd been, on Outdoor Relief. Husband deserted her, see. Sarah Dodds was Class Seven, as I remember. Sick, she was. Needed care. But then they all got put in the Union. And Sarah's kiddies died there. All except a boy who'd run away at the Tasker riot. So Sarah's alone now."

Filled with renewed shame at his desertion of his mother, he urged on his horse. He would stable it at an inn and find this new Union Workhouse on foot. Gaining directions from the ostler, he walked with slower and slower steps to what was, in appearance, a fine stone building. Ringing the Workhouse bell, he wondered what his mother would look like now. And would she want to see him after all these years? After his cowardice in running away?

When the door opened, he asked whether Sarah Dodds was resident there and whether he could see her. The porter asked who he was and the reason for his visit. "I'm – I'm a relative," he explained.

"You're not a reporter? Not from one of them London newspapers?"

"Certainly not! Why should I be?"

"We've been plagued with them, that's why. And with members of Parliament. Wanting to know our business and then putting it in the papers."

"I'm just a relative," Joseph answered firmly. "I want to see Mrs. Sarah Dodds."

Finally the porter asked him to sign the visitors' book and then disappeared. Joseph sat patiently in the entrance hall and looked about him. The building did not appear unattractive and his chair was at least comfortable. But is was the smell that offended him. That, and the silence. If this was a well-run institution surely there should be voices? Disturbed, he moved into a passageway on his right and looked through a window into what he took to be the women's yard. And was appalled.

Old women, wearing the Union uniform dress and with shawls over their heads, shuffled round the open space. Some had sticks to support them while others felt their way along the walls as if blind. All looked weak, undernourished and miserable. Gaunt-faced and thin. Even the younger ones wore a look of apathy and despair, and all had the grey appearance of misery and ill-health. They were so frail he could not think how they were able to remain upright.

When he heard the sound of doors opening and shutting, and the sound of keys being turned in locks, he moved back to his seat. The porter returned, pushing an ancient and toothless woman ahead of him.

"Mrs. Sarah Dodds," was all he said, and then sat down himself, opposite Joseph's chair. This was not to be a private interview, it seemed.

Leading the old woman to the chair beside his, Joseph took one of her gnarled and withered hands in his own. "Do you remember," he began, "a son of yours who went away? About the time of the riot at Tasker's? Your husband was captured, I think."

She raised her head a little and murmured that she remembered. When he reminded her that the boy's name was Joseph, she showed more interest. "That's right," she said. "Never did see him again. Dead, I dare say."

"No, he's not dead." He paused to let her absorb this, adding gently, "My name is Joseph – Joseph Dodds."

She stared at him for a while. "You bain't him?"

He nodded and held her hand more firmly, the tears running down his face.

"Well," she said wonderingly. "You've grown such a lot! I'd never have known you. You was only a nipper when you left."

After a while and many comforting little hugs, he asked the porter if he could see the Master. "I wish to take my mother away from here."

The Master's office was upstairs and Joseph went there alone. He was greeted politely and had no trouble in obtaining his mother's release, although he was required to sign several forms. Having asked the porter to obtain a cab, he took his mother and her small bundle of belongings to the inn where he had left his horse. At first, the landlord was averse to taking in a pauper, still dressed in Workhouse uniform, but Joseph offered to pay double the sum normally charged and a room was soon allocated. He helped his mother up the stairway and into her bedroom where she looked around her with obvious pleasure, smiling for the first time.

"Well!" she said. "This is a treat! Proper bed, and curtains to the window!"

Joseph arranged for hot water to be brought and later a light meal, which she ate while he stayed with her. Not wishing to overtire her on this first and emotional day, he persuaded a chambermaid to help the old lady to undress and into bed, early though it was. Having said a fond goodnight, explaining that his own room was just next door, he went downstairs and ordered himself a meal and mug of beer. While he sipped this he talked to the barman, who was pleased to chatter, there being few other customers at the time.

So it was that Joseph learned about the Andover Workhouse and the great scandal it had caused. The conditions there had been unusually terrible, it seemed, and at last word had leaked out and reached the ears of John Walter, owner of The Times newspaper and the Tory Member of Parliament for Berkshire. Apparently, from the time of the Reform of the Poor Law Act in 1834, he had been against the idea of joining the Parish Poor Houses together to make fewer, but larger, Unions in the towns to house the poor and unemployed. The Government's idea had been to make residence in these Unions so unpleasant that no one would wish to live there. Poverty was to be seen as a sin – and sins were to be punished – and to a large extent the plan worked, for the number of paupers receiving Relief dropped considerably. But for long years the Unions were objects of total dread to the poor.

However, many others beside Walters realised that, in times of genuine hardship, poverty was unavoidable. Harvests could fail; sickness come; industries collapse. Poverty was not necessarily a sin and many, including William Cobbett, another MP, tried to point this out.

Much of this Joseph already knew. He had, after all, taken part in the Swing Riots of 1830 when Tasker's Foundry was attacked, and he had long since understood the reason for that violence. Even down in Dorset he had heard of the Luddites, who had also fought against machinery but earlier in the century and in the more northerly counties of England. He knew of Tolpuddle, a village to the west of Poole, where some farm labourers had formed a branch of the National Consolidated Trades Union in 1834 and been sentenced to transportation for doing so. ("Martyrs", they had been called, and were very much local heroes.) Word had also come to the King Charles Inn, of a People's Charter, set up in 1838 by the London Working Men's Association and submitted to Parliament. This had been largely directed against the 1834 Poor Law Amendment Act which had removed the Outdoor Relief for most paupers, replacing it with entry to the bleak Union Workhouses.

Although Joseph's sympathies were naturally with the poor, he had heard too many discussions among the merchants and ship-masters in the bars of Poole not to know there was another side to the problem.

It seemed that since the collapse of business and prosperity after the Napoleonic Wars, there had been just too many able-bodied men out of work. The old system of Parish Relief could not cope with the numbers it had to support and was, itself, bringing poverty and hardship to the local parish ratepayers who had to fund that Relief. Reform was obviously necessary and had been achieved with general success through the new Union Workhouses, for the Local Guardians were, in the main, conscientious and reasonably humane. It was they who chose the Masters of the Workhouses and who were responsible to the Poor Law Commissioners, appointed by the Government.

Only the Andover Union was a total disgrace. The almost daily articles in The Times, by the special correspondents employed by the owner, John Walters, succeeded in exposing the exceptional brutality, harshness and quite unnecessary cruelty. Unfortunately, the Guardians had appointed a former sergeant-major, Colin McDougal, and his wife, Mary, as the Master and Matron, and these two enforced the law with heartless severity, treating the paupers as if they were dangerous criminals. The barman told Joseph that even during the terrible winter of 1837 and early 1838, when snow lay feet deep over the countryside, with every road blocked and villages cut off, the McDougals had refused to give any kind of aid to a family if the man was able-bodied, despite there being no work available. Many paupers therefore starved to death, or died of cold or pneumonia. The following January of 1839 was even colder. Travellers had said that the River Thames was frozen over for its whole length, and local economies had collapsed. All Workhouses became overflowing with inmates and, at Andover, the rations of food were again cut to the bare minimum, resulting in deaths and disease.

When the weather improved, many thankfully left the Union, preferring to take the chance of finding work outside, risking a cleaner and less squalid death. Sarah Dodds had been one that remained. The dates when her children had died Joseph did not know. There would be records, though, he supposed. He, at least, had come through the worst of the bad times – the 'Hungry Forties", as they were beginning to be called.

"Your brothers and sister would have been taken from your mother, you know," the barman confided. "Children are put in one ward, women in another, and men in another. Mothers seldom see their young ones, and married couples are separated. Don't want no more paupers born in the parish, see. But it's cruel, especially for the old folk. There is no comfort nor loving in that place."

He went on to tell Joseph of the worst scandal of all – the pounding of bones. "Everyone in a Workhouse has to work, even if they're old. Searches out the merely work-shy, see. But it's not easy for the Guardians to think of work for the inmates to do. Here at Andover they hit on the idea of making bone-meal fertilizers, for farmers to put on the fields, and fitted up pounding boxes. Wooden boxes, they are, about a foot in depth and one and a half feet across. Into that are tipped old bones and the workers have to pound them to powder with crushers. Iron, these crushers are, long and very heavy. The littlest boys of nine or ten are stood in pairs on other boxes, 'cos they can't manage otherwise."

He shook his head. "But it's the smell that gets them down. Rancid, those bones are. From the slaughter houses, and such. Green with rot very often, and crawling with flies and maggots. The stench makes people sick but they're kept at the pounding for eight hours a day. They get bad cuts too, from bits of bone flying up into their faces. But they have to let the blood run – aye, and the tears – for they daresn't stop, otherwise they'd never get through the hundred-weight they're allotted each day."

Joseph was appalled at the thought of his mother enduring such treatment. No wonder she was haggard, grey and clearly ill. He was filled with a renewed and terrible guilt at not having rescued her before.

"It was them reporters what revealed it all. Workhouses is open to visitors, so they could go in freely, and they saw the paupers gnawing at those stinking bones and eating bits of old gristle off them. They was so hungry, see. Starving, really, so a rotten piece of sinew was as good as a feast and a nibble of marrow a proper luxury. There've been fights over an inch or so of putrid marrow, so I've heard. Woundings, and all. But when it all got written up in the papers, questions was asked in Parliament and there was a terrible fuss."

He refilled Joseph's mug and leant his elbows on the bar top. "The McDougals are still there, though, but since they was caught up in the scandal I've heard they've turned a bit kinder. They used to thrash the little kiddies if they wetted their beds. And the things they did to young girls who'd been left with bastard babies! Terrible, as I understand. But then McDougal is drunk most of the time. Has relations with the pauper women, too, if they is any way good looking. But now there's to be a public enquiry about it all. Here in Andover it'll be, in front of the Assistant Commissioner for the Poor Law who's coming from London. I just hope the McDougals get turned out and someone half-way decent takes over. Not all the Masters is bad. We've just been unlucky, I guess."

Joseph left the remains of his beer and went out into the street. He needed to walk and to be by himself. The account he had just heard appalled him and he was filled with both anger and mounting self-reproach. The only information he had previously received on Workhouses had concerned that at Blandford, about which there had been no scandal as far as he knew. If he had realized the Andover Union had such a terrible reputation he would have found his mother long since. Stupidly he had thought a Union Workhouse would be as benevolent and understanding as were most parish Poor Houses. He had visualised his mother in a simple but caring environment, well looked after, warm and fed with, perhaps, his brothers and sister later giving her a home with them. Instead, she had endured this horror. Alone.

Turning abruptly, he strode back to the inn. Tomorrow he would take her back to Poole, even if it cost him his last coin to provide a comfortable conveyance for her. From now on she would be loved and cosseted. And she would see his wife and her two grandchildren. For her, the long scandal was over.

Based on:

'Waterloo Ironworks: History of the Taskers of Andover, 1809-1968' by L.T.C. Rolt. David and Charles, 1969.

'The Scandal of the Andover Workhouse' by Ian Struther. Geoffrey Bles, 1973.

'The Victorian Workhouse' by Trevor May. Shire Publications Ltd., 1997.

'Britain Since 1800: Towards the Welfare State' by Howard Martin. Macmillan Education, 1988.

'Early Victorian Britain, 1832-51' by J.F.C. Harrison. Fontana Press, 1989.

'An Illustrated History of Modern Britain, 1783-1980' by Denis Richards & J.W. Hunt. Longman, 1983.

'Changing Britain: 1815-51' by Grey Hetherton. Hutchinson, 1989.

Papers, Documents & Newspaper Reports held by Andover Museum.

Chapter Thirteen

Winchester, 1908

George Clay stood at the window of his living-room and stared unseeingly at the Lower High Street below. He was worried by the realization that Winchester was changing fast and it was no longer acceptable to live above the shop, as he did. His wife, Dorothea, had often told him that he had enough money in the bank to buy one of the new houses on the western hill, beyond the old city walls. He could now, she insisted, move his family to a more prestigious home. Furthermore, their present living quarters could then be used as extra storage space for the merchandise and the ground floor sales area be thus extended.

He knew the economics of the plan were sound; what worried him was his status. Would he, as a tradesman, be seen as a pretentious social climber if he moved into a middle class area? Would his new neighbours, who would almost certainly be from the professional classes, despise him?

Jingling some coins in his pocket, he considered the situation. Now old Queen Victoria was dead, social positions seemed to matter less. With Edward the Seventh on the throne many things had relaxed – not, perhaps, among the titled and rich where class and landowning still mattered, but among ordinary people. In the past there had been several aristocratic and truly upper class families living in the city, but now they had gone. Their grand town houses had been either divided into apartments or pulled down to make way for streets of smaller dwellings, built by property developers for the increasingly prosperous working class.

The matter was really one of the extent of his own ambition. Did he wish to expand his business and move to a new house, where his children could mix with a better type of family and be clear of the disease and squalor of this lower part of the city, or was he content to moulder away as a small tradesman?

He jingled the coins yet again and then turned to his wife. "We'll move," he declared, his mind made up. "I'll have a look at the houses in Weeke. Or Fulflood, perhaps? I don't think we want to be too near the Romsey Road – not with the new Barracks on one side and the County Gaol on the other. Not to mention the Hospital or the Teacher Training College. The prices will be too high in all that area, what with villas and what-not for army officers and prison staff. But we'll find somewhere."

His wife was delighted. "I'm sure we'll be better suited among a higher class of person. The girls need to meet some respectable young men of their own ages."

Edith joined in eagerly. "But not too young, Mother! The younger officers will be just right for Annie and me! They'll make a change from the riff-raff down this end of town!"

"Oh, the snobbery!" exclaimed Leonard who, at eighteen had ideas the family feared were becoming republican. "Don't tell me those stuck-up officers in their fancy uniforms are better men than those from round here – because I won't believe it!" He turned to his parents and, with contempt in his voice, added, "And I suppose that eventually you'll be aiming for those even grander houses on St. Giles Hill? What snobs you all are!"

"But it's our health!" his mother protested. "This really is a bad district for health. It lies too low and too near the river. When your grandmother was alive she remembered seeing the effluent running down the streets – and into the drinking-water wells when the cesspits overflowed! The Brooks area was the worst, she said, and the stench nigh on unbearable. Sometimes she couldn't even open her windows! There were pigstyes nearby, you see. No wonder the hospital was moved from Parchment Street – apparently the overflow from its own cesspit went straight into the water of the Upper Brook. And the wretched people living in the hovels alongside had to use it for washing and cooking – until the pit was eventually cemented over. Yes, I'll be glad to leave here and move to the hillside. Better air; better people."

"Well, we've at least got mains water here now," George added thoughtfully, "but up at Weeke – or wherever we go – we'll have proper sewerage, too. With all these new houses being built they've had to extend the Garnier Road Pumping Station to service them all."

George looked at his family. He was very fond of them. The young ones were all intelligent, both girls working as clerks on typewriting machines, and Leonard in the family business. With his own commercial success and a loving wife, he was very satisfied. So satisfied, in fact, that the next day he began to wonder whether he could put up for Councillor – once, that is, he was living in his new house on the western hill. After all, he was ambitious, forward-looking, owned an expanding business, and was very much a Winchester man. He was even quite well educated. After leaving school he had spent many evenings in study at the Mechanics Institute in the Square. Now, of course, that building had gone and the City Museum was on the site, opened in 1903. The Institute had done him proud and he would have liked Leonard to have gone there, too.

He thought again about Weeke. When the Local Government Act had been passed in 1894 the Weeke area was redistributed into two distinct civil parishes. Maybe he could stand for the larger one, lying outside the City proper? What a good thing the Dean and Chapter of the Cathedral had been allowed by the Church Commissioners to sell off some of their agricultural land! With such an expanding population new housing was urgently required – and, no doubt, new Councillors to represent the occupants.

He would stand as a Liberal, he thought. When younger, he had been deeply impressed by William Budden, the great local Liberal and frequent Mayor. George remembered his funeral – a splendid and truly Victorian affair. Tom Stopher, the architect, then became Mayor and the Liberal leader in the City, followed by Alfred

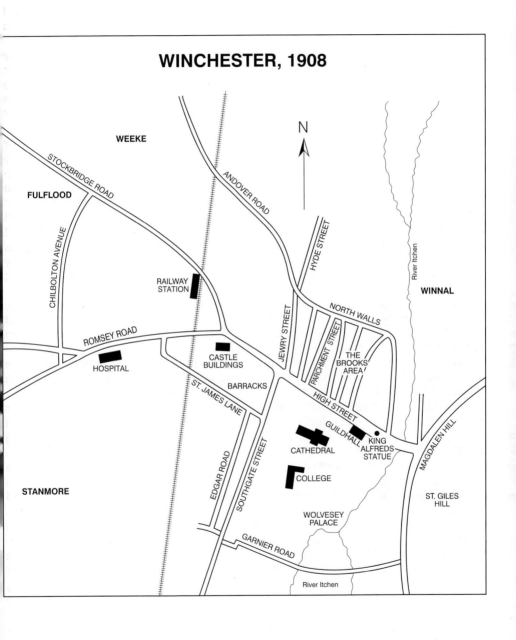

Bowker. It had been Bowker who had organised the erection in 1901 of the bronze statue of King Alfred, crafted by Hamo Thornycroft and now in the Broadway. Alfred the Great's millenary celebrations had been splendid – for the unveiling of the statue the streets had been so packed that he had not let Dorothea or the two girls join the crowds. Instead, they had watched from their upstairs windows, as the great procession came down the High Street after leaving the Council Buildings, passing through the Westgate and so into Broadway. If he remembered rightly, it was led by the Lord Mayor of London, followed by the Lord Lieutenant and the High Sheriff of Hampshire, and then many other dignitaries in their robes. At each corner of the statue tall masts had been erected with garlands at their tops. It was all very decorative but he had impressed on his family that, although King Alfred held his sword high, the point was downwards, indicating that he was both a great soldier and a great Christian, the hilt forming a cross.

Yes, when the time came he would stand for the Council as a Liberal. Definitely not as Labour. That party still seemed too extreme, although at the General Election of 1906 there had been thirty Labour Members of Parliament elected. Anyway, he did not feel that a future resident of Weeke would be welcomed if he was openly in favour of trades unions and socialist societies. He aspired to be of the respectable middle class. He was worried, though, that he did not understand the Liberal arguments concerning Free Trade, Tariff Reform, Home Rule for Ireland, Female Suffrage or topics of that sort. He was no politician, although he knew how to run a shop profitably and fairly, and that was enough for now.

Leonard was a different problem. Eighteen was the age for idealism but sometimes the boy went too far. He and his friends seemed contemptuous of the old ways and wanted political change immediately, regardless of from where the money was to come to fund their ideas. Regrettably they seemed to have little respect for authority or the wisdom of their elders. He worried especially when he heard that Leonard had joined a noisy crowd of young men, led by a painter and decorator called Joseph Dumper.

It was now late May and an angry rumour was circulating that the captured Russian gun from the Crimean War was to be dismantled and removed. It had stood for some years on its low carriage in the Broadway, becoming a favourite place of assembly. Open-air temperance meetings were held there, and the Salvation Army sang their hymns nearby. Now it was being said that the Council had decided that as the Winchester National Pageant was to be performed shortly, the gun should be repainted and the rather rusty railings that surrounded it should be removed. It was felt that as the new statue of King Alfred was so splendid and the Abbey Gardens now so attractive, the gun should be brought up to standard. To this end the railings were to be taken away and the gun to be lifted from its carriage for cleaning.

Unfortunately, this sensible plan did not reach Dumper or his gang, for a few days later a protest meeting was held on the site, with Joe Dumper as the principal speaker. There was a local tradition that the gun should never be interfered with and, once before, there had been a near-riot when this was threatened. That was in June, 1884, which was the seven hundredth anniversary of the Winchester Mayoralty, and the City Council had wanted to remove the gun in order to put up a more relevant monument on the site. The local outrage was such that this plan was abandoned. Now, this evening, he could hear that a similar protest was underway. When speeches had been made and the cheering ceased, Dumper sat on the gun carriage and was dragged about by his boisterous followers to the delight of the gathering crowd.

George Clay, watching from a window of his house, was appalled. Supposing Leonard was among that unruly mob? These were his friends after all. And Joe Dumper – was he of that highly respected family of caterers, Messrs. Dumper and Sons of the High Street? If so, what a disgrace! It almost warranted an abusive letter through the post. But then – if Leonard was also one of that noisy gang, what should he have done to curb his own son?

He had heard from public talk that the railings surrounding the gun had been removed that Monday morning. Apparently, the City Surveyor, acting on his own initiative, had ordered their removal at dawn, so as to avoid his workmen being attacked by angry protestors. They, however, were so infuriated by what they saw as vandalism, that they decided to call a public meeting. This was done by advertising on boards placed in a handcart which was then wheeled about the city.

When Edith and Annie returned from work they reported having seen Joe Dumper driving about in a pony trap with posters fixed to its sides. The meeting was to be held at seven o'clock that evening in the Broadway, to the excitement of the girls.

When the time came, the police, whose office was under an arch below the Guildhall, behaved unobtrusively and did not interfere with the protest. At one point George wondered whether the military had been sent for, as he saw a few soldiers on the edge of the crowd, but they were approached by an N.C.O. from the Military Police and were sent up the hill, presumably back to Barracks. Then a young man appeared with a cornet. He sat on the muzzle of the gun and blew loud blasts to attract everyone's attention. Dumper then stood on its centre and read out the names of nine members of the City Council considered guilty of wishing to disturb the gun. The question was asked as to why the railings were removed at such a very early hour if there were no feelings of guilt about the act. Somebody else complained that, without the protection of the railings, children would vandalise the gun.

Joe then declared that he was going to see the Mayor at his home and suggested that the crowd should accompany him. With more cheers and noisy cornet blasts, Joe was lifted onto the shoulders of some of his followers. Alarmed at the thought of Leonard caught up in such a disturbance, George left the house to find him. Following the rowdy procession, he went along Cross Keys Passage, Silver Hill and into Lower Brook Street. By the time they reached the Mayor's house, there were ten or so policeman, under the command of Head Constable Felton, lined up on the edge of the footway. George saw a few stones thrown by men in Dumper's crowd which smashed some of the Mayor's windows, but when it was announced that the Mayor was not at home, most of the crowd left.

George had still not seen Leonard but, as many of those about him were of the boy's own age, it was not easy to pick out individuals. Continuing to watch anxiously, he followed the others, alarmed that many of the missiles were clearly carried in the boys' pockets and now used to smash the street lamps in North Walls and Jewry Street. Grimly he thought of the cost to the Council for repairs. No doubt the Rates would go up again. The young were so stupid. He had never behaved like this when he was young! England was clearly going down hill – and the so-called Edwardian peace and stability were but myths. Back in the High Street more windows were smashed and the face of the town clock damaged. The whole affair seemed quite pointless. Destruction for destruction's sake. Almost for the fun of it. At every crash of glass the rioters cheered and became even wilder.

When the mob reached Broadway again he hurried to his own house in the hope that Leonard had returned. He was not there.

"But we saw him! We saw him!" Annie exclaimed. "He's following Joe Dumper!"

Grimly George nodded and went out again. The excited crowds were now even larger and seemed to be angry, shouting for the railings to be put back. The police were more in evidence but seemed powerless, for with stones flying in every direction every lamp in Broadway was now smashed and the dusk made things harder to see. George did realise, though, that two of the seats placed for the convenience of pedestrians were being carried away and dumped in the river nearby. One party of yelling youths then set off for the ruins of Wolvesey Palace where a rehearsal of the City Pageant was in progress. Seeing them leave, High Constable Fenton and his men fetched their bicycles and, racing ahead of the crowd, were able to bar the Wolvesey gates. This was without effect, the mob pushing through and then trying to set alight the stands and other woodwork. When this failed they threw about what they could, damaging the rehearsal piano and greatly alarming the bewildered actors. George saw the wooden model of an ancient chariot first burnt and then the remains thrown into the river near the Weirs. After much cheering everyone returned to Broadway and the gun. From somewhere a rope was found and the barrel hauled off and dumped on the ground. This was despite the earlier anger against the Council for planning to do the same thing. The rope was then attached to the empty gun carriage and, with Joe sitting on the frame, it was pulled up the High Street to more shouting and cheering. At the back of the crowd, George had been in danger of being crushed by this sudden surge of bodies but managed to stand clear. After that he went home, only to find Leonard still missing.

"I'm not going out there again!" he declared to his wife. "Those men are mad! Drink must have got into them – although I saw no sign of bottles. The whole thing is a disgrace! The police should send for re-inforcements. Or the military. And why didn't the Mayor read the Riot Act? Disgraceful, the whole thing."

Dorothea did her best to quieten him and he could see she was alarmed by his agitation. Turning to the girls she said crossly, "Come away from the window, now. The excitement's over and you should be ashamed of yourselves, enjoying a scene like that. Edith, make your father a cup of tea and bring it here."

It was only the next day that George managed to find out what had gone on after he had left, for some of his customers were only too eager to tell him. Apparently the mob had returned up the High Street, smashing more windows as they went and this time damaging the figure seven on the town clock. They then turned into Southgate Street and on to Edgar Road, where the City Surveyor lived, and broke four or five of his windows. (A report came out later that his little son's bed had been covered with stones and broken glass but the boy was unhurt, having been in another room.)

Later that evening George heard the shouting of the mob as they came again to the Broadway, so he closed the street windows, drew the curtains and forbade his family to look out. Clearly the situation was becoming more and more dangerous but despite this there was a moment of silence while a man spoke. This was followed by noisy booing, jeers and laughter, followed by more glass smashing. Apparently it was then that the Mayor offered to replace the railings and, even through closed windows, Joe Dumper could be heard calling for quiet while he repeated the offer to the crowd. This had no effect at all, and when the roaring continued, George did move the curtains a little to see what was going on. The Mayor appeared to be pointing to the western hill as if to indicate the army barracks. As he descended the Guildhall steps to enter the Police Office, a large piece of wood was thrown at him but, missing, smashed a window in the adjacent Fire Station.

After a while the military did appear (having been summoned by telephone, George presumed) and the sight of them marching down the High Street was very welcome. In the gathering gloom, now unrelieved because of so many smashed street lights, a man was seen going to speak to their officer. (This, George heard later, was Major Warde, Chief Constable of the County.) After sending the soldiers away, he mounted the Guildhall steps and spoke to the mob. George now eased up the window a little to hear his words. The crowd was told they need have no further concern for the gun, for he had been a Gunner for twenty-five years and Gunners loved their guns. At this the crowd cheered, and did so again when Major Warde explained that although the Mayor could have read the Riot Act, he had refused to do so. More cheers. As it was now nearly midnight, the rioters began to leave. No-one seemed to have been arrested. Thankfully George sent his family to bed, locked the outer door against Leonard, and retired himself.

The next morning his very sheepish son returned, having spent the night with a friend. George took him into his office and berated him severely as a foolish young hot-head.

By evening the Broadway was yet again filled with people – clearly not protesters this time but sightseers, word of the riot having spread. So great were the numbers that Joe Dumper was sent for to disperse them. He explained that the night before the Mayor had agreed to replace the railings and to leave the gun untouched. Three cheers were then given for the Mayor and, as there was clearly to be none of the previous night's excitement, the crowd soon left.

George continued to be distressed, though, and barely spoke to his disgraced son. He was concerned not only with the poor reputation Winchester would now have among the wider public but with the fear that, being the father of a rioter, his future ambitions would suffer. He grumbled to Dorothea that young people were now so discontented.

"It's as if they think they can run the country by themselves – and demand what they like. How, for instance, are they to be given higher wages when we've just been through a financial slump? That Boer War caused a lot of trouble. And we've very little real industry in Winchester to provide the money."

"Unless you can count the visitors and day trippers?" his wife asked. "More and more of them are coming."

George had to agree. "Yes and this year I've put up a new stand of illustrated postcards! Views of the High Street, Wolvesey, Butter Cross, the Cathedral and so on. They're selling very well – as are those little pieces of china with views of Winchester on them. Cheap stuff, really. Just souvenirs. But they do sell."

"And the teashops, don't forget. They bring in the money. As do the Family Dining Rooms. Now that cars are coming as well as the excursion trains, we'll soon be full up with visitors."

"I remember the first car here," George added thoughtfully. "In 1887. A Daimler, it was."

"Also we've many more clothing shops now," Dorothea went on. "Ready-made items – shoes and all. The tailors and cobblers will be going out of business, I dare say. When I remember the hours my mother spent making our clothes out of hand-me-downs and bits and pieces, this seems a different way of life. Not as happy, though. People seem greedier for money, now."

"I can't blame them for that. Life used to be very hard. No end of men out of work. And their families suffering. Now they say this Unemployed Workman's Bill will be pushed through Parliament. It'll give work or maintenance to every one, not just the aged and those of the deserving poor who are not already receiving aid from the parish Poor Law."

"But state pensions?" queried his wife. "They talk about bringing those in this year, but how can the Government afford them? Especially if they bring the age limit down from 70 to 65. There are too many old people altogether."

George grunted. "Put up taxes again, I don't wonder. Where else will the money come from? Asquith will have to do something – he is Chancellor, after all." He pondered this matter for a while. If he was to become a Councillor he would have to consider these problems as well as those of local concern. From now on the newspapers would be studied more carefully.

It was Edith who brought up the subject of the Pageant. She had an interest in history and had been looking forward to seeing the show at Wolvesey. Now she asked whether the disruption caused by the gun riot and the damage done to the stands and piano would delay the production. "I'm sure Mr. Benson is really angry – he's the producer, isn't he? And the Cathedral fund people must be angry, too, for it's all to raise money for the repair work being done there. With the east end sinking into the mud, and all that."

"Can we go to the Pageant?" Annie asked eagerly. "The father of a friend of mine at work is in it, and she's going. Can we, Dad? It'll be on for six days and will be really interesting – the history of Winchester in nine episodes. Special music and costume designs! All the top people in the town are acting. As kings and queens and so on. And my friend says Alderman Thomas Stopher is Sir Walter Raleigh and his speech before he goes to the scaffold makes every one cry. Not her father, of course, but the ladies."

"I think we can go," George replied. "I can't see why not. We have to help the Cathedral if we can. The papers say there's concern for the old building from right round the world. And money coming in from all over. It wouldn't do for we citizens to be laggard with our help."

The girls were delighted, as was Dorothea. Perhaps, George thought, if they do another pageant when he was a councillor he'd be given a part, too – mix with the upper people of the town. So he smiled at his family and said even Leonard could go if he wished.

He thought about the Cathedral – not that he worshiped there himself, being Congregational and attending the new church in Jewry Street, but as Annie had pointed out, a great deal of Winchester's history lay in that building. And now it was crumbling. The scaffolding on the west end had been up for some time but now he was hearing amazing stories about the east end. It seemed the great church had been built on peaty and waterlogged ground near the River Itchen. How it had stood since the Norman days of the eleventh and twelfth centuries he did not know. It was no wonder that its eastern walls were moving and cracking, nor that the crypt was often flooded. He had seen for himself that the south wall of the east end had moved so much that its top overhung the base by up to four feet. The architects now had to put the matter to rights and he had been told that divers had been sent down to shore everything up. William Walker was the chief diver and he had been down in the murk and muck for weeks, underpinning the structure with hundreds of bags of concrete. A horrible job, especially with those tons of cathedral stone above, just waiting to come down.

A week or so later he heard of a house for sale in Fulflood, not far from the Stockbridge Road. It was within his price range and the area would be a definite step up from their present house. And despite Leonard's gibe about snobbery, these things did matter and he could see nothing wrong with wanting to better himself and the family. Perhaps one day he would be able to afford somewhere nearer Stanmore and the developments going up in that district. But St. Giles Hill, to the east of the city, would always be out of his reach. Big houses, they were there. Too grand for him.

After a visit to his bank manager, he did buy the house. Dorothea liked it and the girls were delighted at the thought of not having to share a bedroom. Leonard, of course, made his usual derogatory remarks but George felt he would change his tune once he had experienced the benefits of greater comfort. He was disappointed in this, however. One day the boy announced he would not be accompanying the family to the new house.

"I'm joining the Army," he said. "And when I'm old enough, the Labour Party. All that you lot want to do is to go up in the world – betraying your roots, I call it. But you'll never be real Liberal middle class – you're working class. I want to stay that way, so I'll not join you in your social climbing. I'd rather be honest and stay among my mates. I don't want to mix with your kind of people."

All this was a sadness to his family but there was nothing they could do. So they moved house without him and enjoyed the better air and the cleaner streets on the western hill. Edith and Annie joined the local tennis club and Dorothea took to charity work, but when Leonard had his occasional leaves he did come to join them.

And all the while George worked towards becoming a Councillor. He felt sure he would succeed in this – given time and the necessary diligence.

Based on:

"Winchester" by Barbara Carpenter Turner. Paul Cave Publications, 1998.

"Hampshire with the Isle of Wight" edited by Arthur Mee. Hodder & Stoughton, 1939.

"The Winchester Story" by Barry Shurlock. Milestone Publications, 1986.

"Winchester in old picture postcards" by Sara Dick-Read. European Library, 1993.

"Winchester: A Pictorial History" by Tom Beaumont James. Philimore, 1993.

"City of Winchester: Scraps of Information, Volume 5" produced privately.
Held in the County Library, Jewry Street

"Twentieth Century Britain: Economic, Social and Cultural Change" edited by Paul Johnson.
Longmans, 1994.

"Modern Britain" by Edward Royle. Arnold (Hodder Headline), 1997.

Various record cards, mounted photographs, etc in Local Studies section, County Library,
Jewry Street.

Index